The Clement Valley Mice

Khadijah Abdl-Haleem

Table of Contents

Dedication

For my seventeen children.

Ibrahim, Adam (my boys!) Ismail (who understands the weight of being the eldest), Asiya (who's generous to a fault), Safiya (Spelled with only one 'y' and one 'f'), Ishaq (he is the reason for one of my favorite characters in this book), Hamza (a little boy so polite, he sat through my reading of this story, though I am sure he had better things to do), Mariya (she is my twin), Musa (who loves me fiercely in his quiet way), Hajar (I want to be like her. Determined, never letting her emotions get in the way of her goals), Sara (who at first I deemed too little to add to my dedication, until she smiled at me, her eyes filled with love, before the normative age of socially smiling), Henna (who made believers of us all.) May Allah make her always virtuous. For the first of the runners-up, Haroon, who stoically came to fortify his siblings and had to complete the prophet brother theme, may Allah always make your tongue constant in His remembrance! And for the long-awaited Hafsa, we have been preparing for you for almost half of a decade, alhamdulillah, and welcome! Those of you still yet to be known (may Allah bless you for your love, which has already brought light to my heart) and any other child who happens to read this story (though I may not know you by name, I am very pleased to meet you). All of you helped create this story, and I write it because of you. You are my champions and intended listeners.

Acknowledgments

I would first like to thank Joseph Hayes, who, despite his busy schedule read and edited my book with thoroughness as soon as it reached him.

Uncle Dave, Aunt Mary, Aunt Bernie, and Aunt Noni and my mother also provided necessary feedback and encouragement.

A special thanks to Mr. Demir whose love of my book and his personal stories of his life on a farm earned him a crucial place in my book. Without their support, my book could not be what it is now.

About the Author

Khadija Abdl-Haleem is Palestinian-American, who holds a Bachelor's of Science in Communications from the University of Wisconsin.

She wrote for the Jumuah Magazine and The Zakat Foundation of America. She attended three years of study at Al-Azhar University and The Fajr Center.

She has written for Al-Ahram Weekly in Cairo, Egypt, and currently writes children's stories from home.

Prologue

The dining room was filled with the smells of wonderful cooking. The table was food-laden. Fresh-baked pita bread and bread rolls, Mediterranean salad and cheeses, roast beef, and mashed potatoes. A feast.

But underneath the table, there was another one. Much to the dismay of the household family.

"Look! There's Gus-Gus!" called out the visiting daughter, laughing. Her sister, who could not find the humor in the situation, was mortified.

"I am so sorry! Really this is so embarrassing," the mortified sister said.

The laughing sister, who did not mind the furry creatures and always found most things funny, patted her distressed sister.

"Come on," she said, trying to contain her laughter, "I am sure Mr. Demir understands that we live in the middle of the forest, and mice are bound to get in!"

"Easy for you to say," her sister muttered, "you're going back to your house across the world."

Mr.Demir, their father's boss, was one of the most cheerful guests they had ever had. Despite his general friendliness – or maybe because of it – he was a man with a purpose. Mr. Demir and the father of the Clement Keep household dedicated their energies to helping the needy. They made a whole company help people around the world!

The mice, who, generally speaking, tried to remain out of sight, were aware of the goings and comings of the household. They did live here much longer than the new family. The mice were still studying them. They were different than the previous family. They were different from any people they had lived with before. First, the mice, as they still populated the house, did not feel that scared of them. They had tales from their ancestors that were still told with fondness. In their own way, the Clement House mice were defensive and loyal to this new, confusing family. Of course, mice were never 100% comfortable. But the fact that they had at least twelve generations of family before them who were content to make their life on this secluded property, sheltered by forest and great hills on three sides, spoke well of the new (very confusing) family.

The story that all the animals in this Driftless Region were instinctually born with was that this was a protected piece of land. It was as if even the land itself, never allowing the icebergs to drift onto it, did not allow for the destruction of the animal homes. It only seemed to attract humans who, like the land and the wildlife, wanted to protect and preserve it. The new (confusing) family did hunt, though. But carefully, and only to eat. And never, never baby deer or their mothers. Indeed, they actually nurtured a baby deer and sent it back out! Honestly, their dog (who really is his own story) brought it in when the baby was standing out in the open. *"You crazy little creature, what on Earth are you doing out here?"* Thorin, their old dog, asked. *I don't really know, but can you protect me?* The little deer pleaded. And so, the mice began to draw conclusions about this latest family that put their hearts at ease.

This new family had much history in this sequestered area to contend with. It had always been a proud wildlife land, with little rules besides the just instincts of animals. What a shock for the forest animals of the region when another creation simply appeared! They were called humans. Of course, they had known of them somewhere in the recesses of their minds and animal knowledge. They were sent here by the Greatest Who created them too, but, naturally, the intrusion of the human species gave them much anxiety. The story that was passed down went something like this:

The first people on this land lived in houses made of hide from animals. Actually, the homes were made of tree bark, tree branches, and even grass! Of course, the mice could not live with them; the structures were too small. They did live around the homes, though. The structures provided buffers from the cold wind. Though the homes using animal hyde and tree branches made the animals aware that there must have been a few sacrificed animals and cut down trees to make those homes, they accepted it. Aren't there some animals who eat other animals? Yes, they should be careful to keep safe from those animals, but there was always the possibility that something they did could hurt another animal.

But those people never did anything to ruin where they lived. They honored the space of the animals and never disrupted things. They took a step further and always helped a vulnerable animal. The animals were able to live in relative comfort. They were still always careful but generally content. And so, the animals of the Clement Valley home developed a code: do not hurt other animals or prey on the weak. It became understood throughout the land, the land never touched or hurt by glaciers, that Clement Valley was something of a sanctuary.

They were happy that the family that made homes with sticks and leaves and animal hide was their first introduction to humans. At least twenty-four generations later, they watched another family come and build a home with wood, too, though much bigger. They discovered that with this family's new home, they could live inside the walls! And that human family never allowed hunting in their Clement Valley. But then something sad happened. They saw the old woman and her two children go behind the house on a cloudy day. They hung their heads, held one another, and cried. Things were somber, and food was scarce for many weeks after. The mice talked among themselves about searching for another home.

But then the advent of the new (confusing) family gave their traveling plans a pause, and as we just learned, they began to feel that they did not have to leave now! This family was good! They also had lots of little humans (though the little things were absolutely terrifying, they were very welcome to the idea of mice and mostly everything).

The mice and their progeny passed their ancestral tale down the generations.

The mice developed an attachment to them as they were most likely to be in the proximity of their human inhabitors and live off their unintended/intended generosity. They were a part of their lives; the mice would be there through their ups and downs (they would suffer too, in their downs because there were not that many festivities, which meant not that much food!). As they were naturally very observant for their own safety, the mice could see when the comings and goings of people happened. They could tell, too, if it was sad or happy. But animals understand the need to sometimes move, so they accepted it. Especially Gus-Gus.

Gus-Gus, the bold, hungry, and furry deer mouse, complacently — his mouth filled with bits of bread and cheese — told his buddy, "I told you they love us. Especially that one they told us about, the one who does not mind us."

"You are an idiot!" Jack-Jack said, all riled, nervous, and fidgety (he managed to stuff some crumbs in his mouth, anyway). He was not calm. "They don't love us!" (Jack-Jack was hollering) "And the 'one they told us about' always leaves! They don't know how to get rid of us! These guys are not that smart but aren't completely dumb. At some point, they'll do something, and the sister who doesn't mind us will be gone!"

"Yes," said Gus-Gus. "But the other girls like us, too, and they are sort of in charge. I mean, they clean, anyway."

"All the more reason not to trust them," Jack-Jack said, nervously looking from side to side. "It would make getting food and bedding so much easier if they just left everything alone."

"Listen," Gus-Gus said, putting a scrumptious bit of cheese down (putting food on hold meant he was deadly serious) and looking at Jack-Jack. "Jack-Jack, we've been around enough — watching this family and the families before them — to know they will never get smart enough to be rid of us. We have been here a long while, generations before us, when the older families were definitely harder to get around, and we have generations more to come. Just wait and see."

Back at the table, the discussion continued.

"My sister, I, too, used to live on a farm with many, many animals, and my mother taught me that animals have souls, too!" Mr. Demir said, comforting the distraught sister. He began to laugh and continued.

"Maybe my mother's raising me with the value of acknowledging the souls of animals guided me to value the rights of vulnerable people around us and then form this wonderful connection with your father, subhanAllah!"

Chapter 1: And So the Story Begins

Twelve years later, a mouse tore across the living room in pursuit of the delectable piece of cheese covered in peanut butter.

"They think I can't get that? Do they know who we are?" JJ, the 125th, asked disdainfully as he deftly grasped the peanut butter-covered cheese between his tiny fingers.

"That's it," he said with satisfaction as his prize slid out of the trap. He turned and darted back to safety.

"Oh my God," the woman shrieked. "I can't believe it! Are you doing this right in front of me?!"

Just then, GG ran out from under the couch. "JJ!!! She's right there! What are you doing?!"

The woman looked between the two of them, "What?! My God, are you guys cousins or something?! I swear to God you are the progeny of Gus-Gus and Jack-Jack from a million years ago!"

The mice were at once honored and terrified that she knew who they were.

"Well," said JJ, "we know about her, too. She is one of The Ones Who Loves Us. And she doesn't leave anymore, either!"

"She doesn't seem like she loves us right now," said GG, his face falling.

"Yeah, we're not like 'the adorable jock' the girls were all cooing about: 'Oh, he's so cute, did you see him throwing that nut like a football? His adorable little arms'," JJ said, making gagging sounds.

"And he's barely related to us. That outside mouse who thinks he's all that, and now he's got a fan club, and we have a history here!" GG said bitterly.

JJ hung his head, sharing in the feeling of confusion and hurt. "I don't know why they keep trying to get us killed. We only help them, not waste food."

"At least it's just the interlopers from outside who get ... well ... whatever. But I still feel bad for them a little. It could be one of us, you know," GG remarked pensively.

JJ eyed his cousin.

"Maybe we should expand to other places," he stated, almost nonchalantly.

GG's mouth opened in absolute shock.

"Are you out of your mind?" He bellowed. "You are conceding our right to stay in our home?! We have been here for 125 generations!!!"

"Hey, hey, calm down," JJ said placatingly, "hear me out before you act like I told you to make friends with a cat."

"This better be really good," GG said, glaring daggers at JJ.

Chapter 2: The Strange Turkish Man

A small black car pulled up to the house. Tolkien started barking. Suddenly, he stopped.

"Who is it?" whispered GG.

"Can't tell yet, but whoever it is, they gave Tolkien a treat. I swear that dog would let in an ax murderer if the criminal gave him a treat!" JJ told him.

The two mice scampered to the living room door. The window seat offered many nooks for cover.

The door started to open.

A pair of black shoes stepped over the threshold.

"As-Salamu Alaikum?" The man's voice was robust and cheerful. "Anyone home?"

He began to walk forward into the house but stopped. He started to look around. His gaze traveled to the end of the living room, then back to the door. Then he looked down at the ground. Then the bench. Then further down to the corners. He began to laugh.

"What's he doing?" GG asked, panicked.

"I don't know," JJ answered.

"Hello, my little friends," the strange man told them. "I am Turkish, and I was very well acquainted with your kind when I lived on a farm as a boy!"

The mice were frozen. The strange Turkish man laughed softly.

GG and JJ were still standing as if they were glued to the ground.

"Why aren't we running?" GG whispered.

JJ fidgeted.

"I feel like he's safe," JJ said. Then he jumped slightly. "Oh my God, I think he is the man with the mother from a long time ago they told us about! Look at his eyes. They are kind. Like Mouse Lady."

The man sat on the window seat. Looking at them, he began.

"I took two little mice — please forgive me, I was very young — and tied them by their tails on a little tree. I know you understand me, but please do not be alarmed!"

The two cousins instinctively held their tales, looking at him accusingly.

He began to laugh, holding up his hands in surrender.

"Wait for a moment! Since I was a little boy, I have opened my home to all animals! My mother, God have mercy on her, came out and taught me. She told me to let them go and that they are souls!"

Standing up, he called out to the owners again. Finally, he said, "I do not believe they are here, and I will go back to my home. It is not appropriate for me to go further in without permission."

He walked out but turned to say, "It was a pleasure meeting you!" He left, laughing.

Chapter 3: Moby

"I am insane," thought Moby. "For some reason, though, I think this is the right place to be for all insane animals. They are not normal here."

The dog, first of all, simply stopped barking and was easily distracted. Aren't dogs supposed to defend their people? They did that in Minnesota, anyway. For heaven's sake, even his master's parrot would have defended his house better than that dog! His master did not know he was his master, in his defense. Moby jumped into his coat pocket to escape Toby, the parrot. The mice in the house were talking about the dog like they were friends. The horses were curious creatures, too. They just remarked to each other that his master's car was not normal and then continued eating. The only one that was mildly normal was the goat. She told the dog he should dog-up once in a while. But still, why was she talking to him like they were siblings?

But Moby had a bigger problem now. Clearly, something was out of the norm in this already abnormal situation. He had to figure out how to delicately insert himself.

Moby was sitting on the window seat his master sat on. His size was conducive to slipping in and out of places and pockets.

In this new environment, though, he felt hesitant. He decided just to walk over. He began tracing their steps. But there were none! They seemed kind of in a trance-like state. Strange. He shrugged. They were only mice. Bigger than him. But his owner liked them. He took a step. It was a very, very difficult step. He climbed down the window seat. They were only about ten steps in front of him.

There was a carpet on the wooden floor, so the patter of his feet was silenced. As soon as he moved across the floor, the mice snapped to attention. One of them began to fidget almost violently. The other touched his shoulder. It had a calming effect. By this point, the newcomer stood right in front of them.

"Hi. I'm Moby," the little mouse squeaked, staring at them. JJ and GG were dumbfounded.

"That's it??" GG exclaimed.

"Who are you?" JJ felt the need to remain calm.

"Oh, I'm just a little mouse." Moby's little shoulders were straight. JJ couldn't tell if it was from anxiety or from determination. For some reason, Moby seemed like he knew what he was doing.

"Yes, that is clear!" GG did not bother controlling his irritation.

"I am escaping parrots," Moby stated. Clearly, he felt that escaping parrots was a normal thing. "Well, that explains everything," GG said. JJ shoved GG, stopping him from making another sarcastic remark.

"Where will you stay?" GG asked, forcing his face to relax.

Moby fidgeted. "Here?" His statement was a nervous question.

"Of course, he will stay here!" JJ's voice was (mildly) welcoming.

Moby heaved a sigh of relief. "You will hardly notice me!"

"That won't be that hard." GG looked down at the tiny mouse. He did not like change. Though, at least it wasn't a threatening change. He shrugged his shoulders. "Just find a place."

To JJ's and GG's surprise, Moby dashed to the fireplace. The cousins looked at each other, astonished.

"You can't say that he doesn't fit right in with us!"

Chapter 4: The Jock

"Call me Jake," the football player grinned, exuding confidence. "Or, if you prefer, Mr. Adorable like the house ladies call me."

"You are utterly infuriating, peasant," Mr. Knightley grumbled, "and stop making so much noise!"

"Listen, Batguy, your stealthy gliding around the air has caused more noise than I ever do, so stop being all high and mighty, and listen to me!"

"Well, I never!" Mr. Knightley huffed.

Jake snorted derisively.

"Dude, you take yourself too seriously. They only call you Knightley because they are trying to be clever."

"No," Knightley said confidently, "It is because they *are* clever. And I am special."

The disgruntled football player threw his acorn forcefully. No one put him out of sorts like the illustrious bat."

"I don't know why you are so certain of your place here. You are not even an accepted household creature!" The jock clearly had no problem expressing himself.

The bat took a silent turn about the room, chuckling.

"Who are you trying to fool, my little rodent? They are trying their very best to be rid of you and yours," Knightley said.

Jake settled his acorn under his arm.

"Listen," Jake said seriously. "I know the progeny are planning something, and we must figure out what to secure our places here. I am Mr. Adorable and have been saved, and you have a special status for some strange reason."

"Quite true," Knightley said, equally smug.

"But," Jake continued, "we are only barely recognized as that by the family, which is not enough. We need the Originals behind us if we are going to survive here."

"My dear boy, you are my legs that walk me through the narrow passages with my maimed leg and torn wing," Knightley added, drolly, "and you are fettered to a dark closet where you only leave to bring me fruit."

"Oh, believe me, I understand all that and only do it because it is usually near the cheese, which is what I live on. It's such a great thing that one of the Owners here has such mousey tastes," Jake said. Heaving a relaxed sigh, he tossed his acorn up.

"Yes," Knightley said, furrowing his maimed wing, "and such mousey gathering habits. It's rather alarming. No wonder none of the mice in the house infringes upon her gatherings."

"Dude!" Jake exclaimed in near horror. "That's like a sacred law! We don't deal with one of us wrongly. She understands our ways and lives them! She's a surrogate mouse."

"That does not make it any less alarming. Although I do become vexed when they say she's like a squirrel. Disgusting, arrogant creatures," Knightley said, cradling his mangled leg.

Jake looked sympathetically at the bat.

"Sorry, Batguy, that was harsh, what you went through," Jake said, "but it is cool that you don't hold it against them."

"I am older and wiser than you young, inexperienced creatures. I am twenty years old and have seen much of humans and the world—"

"Dude!" Jake interrupted, "Would you knock it off!? You are so full of it! Plus, you give the same speech at least every other week, except usually it starts with 'Bats are the second hugest group of mammals, and I am from the very illustrious group called the Chiroptera order,' and you know

I am quoting you because I would never come up with the word illustrious unless it was from you!"

"Someone has to teach you!" Knightley said defensively. "And I am in the perfect position to do so."

"What, hanging upside down?" asked Jake, playfully poking the bristling bat.

"Well," said the bat, resignedly accepting his ward's affectionate — though slightly uncomfortable — gesture. "In the end, she is their mother, and mothers are precious things that deserve respect, even among us bats. And they were never forceful or aggressive when they directed me out. But I wish they would get a dog that terrifies the squirrels away."

"Tolkien is the chickenest dog in Caninedom, but don't forget how that works for us," said Jake.

"Yes, indeed," Knightley said firmly. "If it weren't for the fact that I despise his languidness, I might actually like him."

"To each his own, in Tolkien's words, right?" asked Jake. "That's good in farm life."

Chapter 5: Introducing Tolkien

Tolkien stretched out across the newly swept storage room. Not that he really cared if it wasn't cleaned. No, he had a higher purpose. If the right opportunity provided itself for him to relieve his boredom, he could lunge into the forbidden house. Actually, it gave him a semblance of human connection. He was a family kind of guy in many ways, though chasing the chickens and tossing them about gave him the same sort of connection. But, at the end of it all, he loved no one like he loved his boy. His boy loved him ferociously. He gave him affection and love only Tolkien experienced. No one else could see it.

He loved all of them, actually. They were his pack. He looked out for each of them in their own special way. He agreed with Mice on one thing. The girls were kind of in charge, and they had his back. He also liked that the mice or the girls did not serve as a threat to his boy.

But Tolkien did have one minor problem. The part of the family that would leave to another place (he was curious to know what opportunities it had in the food way) smelled of Cat. They talked about her enough. They also encouraged the family to bring it to catch the mice. But luckily, Mouse Lady (really, she was as fidgety and nervous and unimposing as the mice. His dog instincts compelled him to watch out for her) was allergic to cats. She had no idea how much that raised her in his esteem.

He laid languidly, not hungry or bored enough to push his way into the house, when the door opened for a second too long. He yawned and thought drowsily, *"I have to find a way to tell the mice about the cat..."*

Chapter 6: JJ's Reasoning

"I will never be able to figure out two things," said GG, fidgeting nervously. "One, how does the sensitive little boy become our worst nightmare? And two, how Alpha (He was just the father, and he was actually pretty nice) saves bugs but has the little boy go against his instinct and set the traps."

"I know! Do you remember when the little boy kept saying, 'I feel horrible, I feel terrible,' when he saw the outside mouse only halfway caught?" JJ said, recollecting the horrible scenario.

Moby shuddered.

"That almost makes me think living with birds is better!" he said.

"I remember better how he tried to put it out of its misery and was truly horrid," GG remembered morosely.

"You have to forgive him. He is only taking orders. And when he saw that disgusting chipmunk being tortured after he accidentally tortured the mouse," JJ added, in defense of the poor boy, "it ruined the movie for him."

"It ruined another mouse's life," Moby said. He bent his head, pained for a fellow mouse.

GG shook his head. "We are in a conundrum. We are almost ruined!"

Curled up in a comfortable crevice in the inner hollow of the wall, JJ calmly told his cousin, "We just have to be clever enough to outwit them. We'll get there. We just have to be patient."

GG began shedding. "Easy for you to say!"

"What? GG, that makes no sense," JJ snapped.

"Yes, GG, JJ has a point. He is in the same exact situation," Moby paused. "So am I, now that I think about it."

GG, naturally, did not appreciate Moby's commentary. He was still getting used to him. He turned to JJ.

"JJ," he said, "you can't just say, 'We'll just have to be patient' when you haven't even talked about your crazy idea of 'expanding' to other places."

"Hey, I did say hear me out, didn't I? I still hold by my advice to be patient," JJ laughed when GG stomped off.

Chapter 7: The Mission

"Now," said Jake, "we need a plan, and since you are so educated, what do you think?"

"Flying does lend me a view that leads to a more complete understanding," Knightley said, nodding his head in pride, stating what he believed to be irrefutable.

"Hey, you know what the owners call what you just did?" Jake stated, snappish and annoyed.

"They call it humble bragging. No wonder you have no friends but me!"

"Come, come, my earth-bound, short-sighted friend. I have many bat friends," Knightley said, "and the two of us complement each other!"

Sitting against the closet wall, Jake was throwing his trusty hazelnut up and catching it, restless and bored.

"Well," the irritable mouse said, drolly, "from your lofty height, what does your 'complete understanding' show you that differs from my honestly humble perspective?"

"Humble?" Knightley scoffed, "You, my dear friend, are the farthest thing from humble!"

"Well," said Jake, grinning and tossing his hazelnut, "you gotta own your worth, ya know!"

"Upstart!" Knightley exclaimed, smiling fondly, "From my lofty perspective, I have noticed something you probably have as well, ground-dweller though you are."

"What?"

"The family has two parts, and they move back and forth between the two places. So, what if we propose that we will go, or rather, you will go, into one of the leaving cars, to see what options the other home adds."

Jake stopped tossing his ball.

"Well, that's an idea," he said thoughtfully, caught between terror and a rush of excitement he hadn't felt since his first adventure coming to this home. "But how do we let them know of our idea?"

"That is where one of your cheese stops comes in," said Knightley. "You know where they hole up, right?"

Jake stood up, "I guess I do."

"Why the long face?"

"Well, I've never actually talked to any of them. They kind of just let me do my thing," Jake said nervously.

"Come now, what is the worst they can do besides refuse?"

Jake plopped down again. "I don't know. Kick me out?" he said uncertainly.

"They can't do that!" Knightley laughed, "Don't forget, I did hear them. I think it was JJ saying maybe they should expand. This is exactly what they are asking for. Mice always have an evacuation plan."

"Are you sure? You know the echoes you depend on; sometimes, they could be inaccurate."

"Never," said Knightley coldly.

"Oh, come on, don't be like that. It's just my nerves talking. It is terrifying to leave this place and see new things. Remember what happened to me when I first came? Or better yet, what happened to that tribe of outside mice in the car?"

"Absolutely horrifying," said Bat, shuddering. "They were very ill-educated, gypsies of a sort. We have the benefit of education. And you were extraordinarily uneducated before you had the benefit of learning from yourself." Knightley, as usual, was very self-assured, and Jake, as usual, was very irritated.

"That is true, but we aren't nearly as educated as the Originals," said Jake. After he finished glaring at Knightley, he let his eyes fill with anxiety.

"But we are going to them, and we are on the same side as them, and they surely will guide us through. Do not forget that we do not come empty-handed," he added, sagely ignoring Jake's glare. "They stand to benefit."

Chapter 8: The Visitor

The moon's light seeped through the tree branches and into the window, casting a peaceful glow in the quiet room.

Well, almost quiet.

"JJ, do you hear that?" GG asked in a frenzied whisper, his ears twitching.

There was the sound of little paws trying to find crevices to maneuver on the cold, stone wall.

"It's just the jock on his normal cheese run," JJ murmured sleepily.

"No!" GG exclaimed staunchly, at this point nearly bouncing off the ground. "It's too early, and it's not the right place!"

"GG, would you relax? We heard them planning to talk to us. I told you to be patient, remember?" JJ could not hold back a satisfied smile. "Thank God for hollow walls! It makes us as good as bats hearing echoes."

"Yes," said GG, "all the more reason to mistrust the jock. One of our own consorting with a flyer!"

"Honestly, you cannot say we took him into our own fold, plus he did nurse Knightley back to health."

"Well," said GG, petulantly, "we let him gather food without so much as a word of objection."

JJ eyed GG with a mild accusation. "We don't have the right to object, as you well know."

"He makes me nervous," GG said defensively.

"You mean he makes you jealous," JJ corrected his sulking cousin.

"What?" GG nearly shouted. "Jealous of what? His unholy relationships with animals he shouldn't have in the first place?"

"His arm, for starters," JJ said, his eyes drifting shut. "That vermin can throw! He has dibs on every hazelnut that comes his way. *Crack, crack, crack,* and he never misses!"

"Well, why don't you move upstairs then and rent a corner of his closet!" GG said bitterly, turning his back on his oh-so-reasonable cousin.

JJ opened his eyes, laughing. "Oh, stop. Leave him alone already. And your arm is not so bad, cuz! You've cracked a nut a time or two! Oh, that's right, those nuts are already shelled!"

JJ began guffawing. Naturally, GG did not share in his humor.

Glaring at his cousin, he told him in biting words, "JJ, we definitely do not know the bat, and there is nothing wrong with being careful!"

Chapter 9: The Meeting

The jock walked carefully in the dead space between the roof and the ceiling. His heart was thumping. Tonight was different. His normal, well-versed path from the closet floor into the space between the hollow walls and the kitchen was not his goal.

Though the house did not seem unusually big to the humans who lived there, it was a maze of incongruent spaces for the mice. The closet Jake and Knightley called home shared a wall with the room, another large room containing a sitting space with a table, a chimney, a door to outside, and the stairs. The mice ran inside the walls and ceilings where the holes were plentiful and gave them free access to the entire house. But the tracks had to be learned.

He was venturing into an unknown area, and it was terrifyingly dark. He closed his eyes and recollected Knightley's instructions: "Now, my brave adventurer, you will not turn right when you traipse across the dead ceiling space. You will turn left."

He muttered to himself, "Not right, left, that's easy enough, isn't i—Ahhhhhhhhh!"

While repeating the words, he fell through a hole in the ceiling onto a bed of shrieking people. Only remembering the instructions, he darted left and ran back instinctively to his safe haven.

"I am so sorry," Bat said wryly, stroking his wing, "I forgot to tell you to watch where you were going."

Jake buried his head in his hands in embarrassment.

"I was so scared, I wasn't thinking straight, and then they were like a pack of howling coyotes! I swear I am going to have a heart attack! Screaming is not good for mice hearts!"

Knightley let go of his wing and bellowed with laughter.

"Then, my friend," he said between breaths, "you are certainly living with the wrong family!"

"Hey, there was that time I ran over Mouse Lady's foot, and she did not let out so much as a peep!" Jake said, lifting his shoulders defensively.

"Well, she is different, and few are like her. Well, except maybe the mother of that strange Turkish man who visited. Maybe his mother was even better, as she was vocal with her son," said Knightley. "Our Mouse Lady here has all the right instincts but just keeps to herself a little too much."

Jake paused his fretting.

"Do you mean Moby's strange Turkish man who showed up at the door? Yeah, his mother was a total, real mouse supporter. Man, she stood her ground. God rest her soul. She was a hero!

Little boys are a natural menace, and their uncontrolled, experimental natures are disastrous!"

Knightley chuckled fondly.

"You must admit it was amusing that he tied them by their tails to the branch. Very scientifically sound."

"I can't say that I am amused," said Jake, holding his tail protectively, "but I will say she is forever remembered by mice all over the world for dealing with us as creatures with souls and rights, even in the face of a little boy."

"Her voice has the strength of a proud, Godly lineage. And look at how good her upbringing turned out! That overly curious little boy grew up as a wonderful man who helps people!"

"That's true. You can even say that saving mice opened his eyes to helping people," Jake said.

"All of that does not mean, my little friend, that when a mouse drops onto your pillow, that does not naturally elicit a scream. One per person. You must admit that the number of pitches that assaulted my sensitive bat ears was as traumatizing to me as you dropping from nowhere for them."

The jock stood, glaring at Bat.

"Okay, there were at least three words I did not understand in that fancified speech, but I understand that your emotional intelligence should match at least fifty percent of your hearing capacity!"

"Fancified! Hearing capacity! Good mouse, you are learning slightly more elevated speech patterns. There is hope!" Knightley said, nodding placatingly.

Jake took a deep, calming breath, "Alright, let's try again."

''Let us go over the blueprint of the house again," said Knightley, with what Jake thought was infuriating patience.

"First off, what is a blueprint? And second, how do you know what it is?"

Knightley gathered his wings to himself and shifted his wounded leg. "I have been around long enough—" Knightley began to drone.

"Oh, come on! I know you are ancient. No need to go on about it!" Jake exclaimed in protest.

Bat continued on unruffled. "I have been around long enough to have caught conversations of the people, and a blueprint is a map, so to speak, that humans use to build their particular type of nest."

"And?" retorted the mouse impatiently.

"Well, the original builder and his wife did not build this home according to any recognized standard, which in essence made this home perfect for us non-humans. It is filled with holes."

The mouse stared at Knightley, slightly open-mouthed.

"So," Jake began, brimming with irritation, "I have just fallen through one of those holes the builder left because he doesn't know what he is doing by any normal standard, and we are in a rush, and now is the time you choose to veer off plan to talk about another bogus plan that has nothing to do with our goal?!"

By this point, Jake was hollering.

"Calm down," Knightley said. "I am giving you background information, and you did ask what a blueprint was, so I told you!"

Jake lowered his head in defeat. "Alright, so now can we go on?"

"We said we would leave, and you dropped down the hole because you weren't looking. So now, watch where you are going and go left." Knightley finished and crossed his wings over his chest.

Jake groaned, "I swear you are trying to punish me!"

"Walk the path again and go left. You will walk for about ten feet, crossing above the staircase. And then turn left again. At this point, you will go down the wall, and you should see the inside of the fireplace, which is made of brick," said Knightley, stubbornly refusing to acknowledge the mouse's grievances.

Jake drew a breath. "Bricks are a relief," he told Bat as he began the path once again.

He scampered up the inside of the wall, muttering to himself what he was thinking about his friend. "Conceited, infuriating, irritating know-it-all. I hate that he is mostly right!" he conceded as he jumped onto the ceiling floor, slightly out of breath.

Watching the ground, he walked carefully. He felt the inner scaffolding begin to change, and the hollow space beneath his feet seemed deeper.

"I must be over the stairs," he muttered, trying to calm his thudding heart.

"What's the big deal anyway?" he told himself as he walked as quietly as he could, waiting to feel the wall become brick. "They're just normal mice." He did not believe himself for a minute. They were the Big Guns.

Finally, the pliable material of the wood changed into an empty space. The jock gasped as he lost his grip and wildly threw his feet around, trying to find any stronghold.

"The single most important direction," Jake squeaked, "like, 'by the way, you will run into a canyon when you get to the fireplace.' Mr. I've been around for so long forgot to warn me? It's 'cause he can fly!"

He found, gratefully, that if he extended his legs, he could reach the outer edge of the rock. There was enough space for him to secure his grip. Between the rocks, if he moved his feet around carefully, there were spaces big enough to comfortably walk. Suddenly, he froze. He heard chatter. His ears perked up, and he began to make out words.

"We just have to be clever enough to outwit them. We'll get there. We just have to be patient. Anyway, GG, would you relax? We heard them planning to talk to us. Thank God for hollow walls!" JJ said, chuckling. "It makes us as good as bats hearing echoes."

Jake's heart dropped in fear. It began sinking in. He was really doing this. These were the mice he had been planning to talk to.

He took a deep breath and continued on his downward path. It was roughly fifteen feet down to the holding of the originals. The voices became clearer and clearer until he was standing right outside where the conversing mice were. He just had to garner the courage to take a step to the right and through a very well-used entranceway.

Chapter 10: The Conversation

With a little prodding from JJ, GG stopped fretting and gathered his wits. He could hear the rapid breathing just around the entrance wall.

"Well," he thought, *"at least I know Mr. Adorable is nervous."* And then, hearing his own thought, felt like a terrible creature. *"What kind of mouse does that make me? And just because he has a great arm that I cannot really compare to."* He was determined to make an attempt at honorable mouse-code behavior.

He breathed in, slowing his heart rate, and turned the corner. He eyed the jock. He was a fine-looking mouse. Relatively tall and healthy looking. GG's noble intentions suffered a little bit.

"Well, finally, we meet!" He tried to make his voice welcoming, charming, and glad. At least he thought he did.

"Oh. Well, yes. We did." The ill-concealed anxiety in GG's voice made Jake a little more nervous.

"I don't usually come this way," the jock continued, as matter-of-factly as he could (GG's anxiety made him wary).

"No, you don't," GG concurred, nodding his head. "What *does* bring you here?"

"Well, well, let us not beat around the bush," came another voice, with a genuinely friendly lilt.

"We did manage to hear you and Knightley discussing a proposition. But let's share a bite of cheese together before we talk. We want to get to know one another! It is not every day we have a guest, so to speak." He finished with a smile.

The jock breathed an audible sigh of relief. He felt much more at ease with this one. The other one, well, he was very jittery and not quite so sure of himself. And not quite succeeding in being welcoming, though he was trying.

Jake entered the home of JJ and GG.

"Nice!" said Jake enthusiastically. There were two hay beds and a plate made of a leaf, with cheese and bits of bread.

"Please, make yourself at home," said GG, becoming more comfortable in the presence of his cousin and in his home.

"Tell us," JJ said as he took a bite, "a bit about yourself."

Jake began clenching and unclenching his fists, missing the feel of his trusted hazelnut. All of a sudden, he saw something coming at him out of the corner of his eye. He twisted, and lo and behold, an acorn flew at him.

"Woah!" he said, laughing in surprise as he caught the acorn effortlessly.

"Nice throw! And, also, how did you know?"

A compliment from the jock himself? GG's heart filled with near instantaneous love. If he could blush, his fur would be stained red.

"Thanks," GG said, "I know your hazelnut is a security blanket for you, and you were fidgety."

"Well, nice deduction, Sherlock!" said Jake.

"What?" said GG, looking puzzled.

"Who's Sherlock? And wow! Now I see what JJ was talking about!" Moby squeaked. He had just climbed up from the fireplace and immediately entered with the jock's fan club.

Who is this? Jake wondered.

JJ and GG scrambled around, trying to make a place for the little (sort of uninvited) mouse.

"This is our new friend," JJ stated.

"He just came," GG added.

"Welcome," Jake said, "but it is weird because I should be welcoming you. I just barely met these guys for real, sans echoes!"

"Two new mice to add to the Clement Valley Mouse clan!" JJ spoke, spreading his arms wide.

"So, who is Sherlock, anyway?" GG asked.

"They even made a mouse character made off of him," said Jake. "He was a detective in a storybook the family who lives here is obsessed with."

"They made a mouse based on him?" asked GG, smiling.

"I told you the humans love us. They can't seem to escape it!" said JJ smugly.

"But it's very confusing because they are always trying to kill us!" Moby was comfortable enough with his new home to include himself in 'us'.

"Well," said Jake, "as Knightley told me, humans can be very puzzling creatures."

"Your relationship with this bat is puzzling to us," said GG, in a mildly accusing tone of voice.

"How on earth did that relationship happen?" JJ asked.

"Are bats anything like parrots?" A wide-eyed Moby asked.

Jake began tossing the acorn up, catching it, and keeping his eyes only on the moving acorn as he started talking. This new, tiny mouse was a total mystery to the jock. He was an unknown in an already unfamiliar situation. At least he was not a real threat.

"Well," he began, "I happened to be outside the parents' room, I didn't know that at the time, but I was there, and the door opened, and people were talking loudly and screaming, and two of them started to direct something out with a broom.

"Now, right in front of the room, there is a pretty big, fenced piece of land. It begins to incline a hill, turning into a forest. At that time of night, it is so black, and who knows what kinds of creatures are hiding in the trees! And then an owl began to hoot, and my blood froze, and I was terrified."

GG, JJ, and Moby sat, staring, riveted. At long last, their curiosity was being relieved!

"They kept saying, 'Be careful, be careful!' So, when I looked, I saw them let go of whatever it was, and then it started to fly! So, while watching this creature fly — My instincts told me at that point it must be a bat — I saw something move under the patch of weeds in front of the door. I got startled because there were a million and one creatures that would love to have me for dinner, and the forest was so dark, and my limbs were not cooperating. I saw it was a squirrel."

He shivered at the memory. "But I shouldn't have let my guard down in the first place just because I assumed they are usually never awake at night. Of course, that usually means something is wrong and should have caught my attention. I was so frazzled, and my mind was not functioning normally. It turns out she was a mother and her babies were hungry, and the food was not plentiful because it had been an abnormally cold week. When they pushed Bat out, his leg got caught in the thorns of the broom. Bats' legs were weak, so his legs broke, and he couldn't fly well. Suddenly, that squirrel lunged up and began to grab at him. I had an acorn in my hand, and I threw it at her with all my might, and she let him go."

At this point, the excitement was at a pitch point.

"That is awesome!!!" GG shrieked.

"You are not only a football player but a genuine hero! You do the name of mice good!" JJ said proudly.

"I always hated squirrels!" GG added.

Jake laughed, internally aglow at the praise of the Originals, "I know you would have done the same."

"I am not nearly so certain," said JJ, laughing softly.

"I know I definitely would not have. I would have hightailed to the nearest burrow!" GG said, simply content to be in such daring company.

"And I would have jumped into the nearest pocket," Moby added. The other mice looked at him, puzzled. When Moby did not explain his comment, they turned their attention back to Jake.

"So, then I had to let Knightley know I was on his side, and I can tell you, he is not so easily convinced. About anything." Jake finished.

"Yeah, we heard him talking about how he comes from an ancient family, who is educated, and that he has a better worldview because he flies," said GG. His voice was filled with condemnation.

"I wonder what he thinks about parrots," Moby wondered aloud.

Jake looked at the tiny mouse and wondered about Moby's infatuation with parrots.

"Well, you will have to ask him that question. I can't be sure," he told Moby. *That might be an interesting conversation,* he thought. *Could go both ways.*

"GG, you must learn to stop being so quick to judge and condemn! Clearly, he has a perspective that we can never have, if for nothing but his age," he said.

"Alright, alright," said GG, begrudgingly.

"You know, guys," Jake said, his voice at once eager and defensive. "Knightley is a pretty standup guy. I think you would like him."

The Originals eyed him questioningly.

"Will we ever have the honor of meeting him?" JJ asked.

"Well, you know, it is kind of hard for him to fly downstairs," said Jake. He paused and then said tentatively, "Maybe you could come upstairs, and I'll do the introductions."

The Originals and the newcomer looked at each other.

"Really?" whispered GG.

"Ahh. Well, I think it is only appropriate for us to go to him with a direct invitation," JJ said thoughtfully. *"He is a bat; they are proud creatures and deserve a certain amount of respect."*

Jake stared at JJ open-mouthed.

"Oh, no way!" Jake said, jumping up. "The last thing Bat Guy needs is that kind of encouragement."

He paused, genuinely surprised, "So it really is true that bats are special."

"So, you don't know about animals and their stations," GG said.

"Oww!" GG cried out when JJ nipped him.

"And you really don't know anything about being polite!" JJ rebuked GG. "You should definitely be afraid to meet Mr. Knightley."

"And none of you guys know anything about parrots," Moby said.

The three mice eyed him warily.

"No, we don't," said JJ. *For some reason,* he thought, *I don't believe Knightley will take to parrots well.*

Jake looked between his three new — possible — companions with intrigue. He actually liked these guys!

"Alright," he began, "I think we should head upstairs. Wait, do you ever go up there?"

GG bristled. "We have been living here for one-hundred—"

"Good Lord, GG, calm down!" JJ interrupted his cousin in exasperation. "Forgive my ill-mannered cousin Jake. He never knew his mother and therefore was not raised with any sense of control."

Jake began to laugh.

"I can tell you, JJ, Knightley will like you. And he might find your cousin acceptable because you keep him in line," he said, winking at GG.

"So," GG began, fixing his posture to hide his embarrassment, "how are we going to do this?"

"Okay," Jake said as he got up. "Just follow me."

"No," JJ said, interrupting. He had a smile on his face, "you follow us! We have, after all, been here for one-hundred-and-twenty-five generations."

"Hey! That is not fair. How come you get to say it?" GG complained.

"Because the time was right, and I knew it would bother you," JJ said, laughing.

"Alright," Jake said, "really, let's go. Do the two of you ever stop bickering?"

"NO!" They said in unison and began scampering up the rocks.

"I can attest to that," said Moby

"Whoa!" Jake exclaimed. Admiration colored his voice as he followed quickly. "I am sure I would have figured this out, but I never come this way."

"Of course," JJ said. He could not help smirking.

Then he frowned thoughtfully. "Actually, you probably would have. You are quick like that."

"Please, don't outdo yourself praising me," Jake said. He joined in the friendly banter of the cousins easily.

The top of the rocks led to a wooden ledge. They toppled over, landing on an oddly spongey surface.

"You know when they overcrowd the table upstairs," remarked Jake as he found his footing. "They have the best food!"

"Yes," said JJ, standing close to Jake. "We know there must be a massive amount because usually, we don't hear you coming down for a day or two. Well, not that we don't come up here to get our share of party food," JJ said.

"I just ate scraps after the birds at my house," said Moby.

Moving his tail back and forth, GG said, "That is terrifying."

"Well, put it in perspective, buddy-old-pal," JJ said, clapping his cousin on the back. "We eat scraps after children, who are equally terrifying!"

"So now what, our new friend?" asked JJ.

"We have to go in one at a time. I can only imagine the havoc it would cause if the three of you went traipsing across the living room," said Jake.

"If anyone saw us, they would mention The Three Blind Mice," said GG, shuddering.

"Horrible story, no regard for our feelings!"

"Dude, they set mouse traps. Of course, they are not sensitive about our feelings!" Jake pointed out dryly.

The four mice stood silently, thinking about that harsh reality.

"Well," said JJ, shaking off the dreadful pall that had come over them, "Jake, you go first, on the ground, and tell Knightley about us, and then we will follow shortly."

"Alright, but give me at least three minutes," said Jake.

"But no more than three! It is dangerous for us to stay out here too long!"

Jake stood at the box's edge, ready to jump down.

"Just blend in with the contents!" He said. He silently hit the floor.

Jake ran as quickly and quietly as possible, turning left when he saw his room door. Flattening his body, he slipped into the room and quickly ran to the closet, sliding in.

"Knightley," he whispered.

"Oh, stop that confounded whispering, boy," Knightley said. "What do you mean bringing them up here to meet me? Am I a showpiece?"

"Don't get all rattled, Pops," said Jake. "Trust me, you will like them. Well, two of them for sure. Plus, you can explain things better than I do. They wanted me to give you fair warning that they were coming before they came."

"My," said Knightley. "That is rather polite for uneducated mice."

"And that is quite rude for someone ultra-educated," said Jake. "Don't forget, what they lack in education, they make up for in family seniority,"

"Two of them, at least," Jake muttered under his breath.

"Well," said Knightley, begrudgingly. "Show them in then."

"Hello?" JJ said. His voice emitted politeness as he stepped into the room. "Mr. Knightley, can we come in?"

"But of course," Knightley answered. He was greatly pleased with the show of manners.

"Please, consider yourself at home. It is, after all, your home!"

Knightley chuckled at his own joke. Jake grimaced.

"Knightley," he mumbled, "please don't try to be funny."

"I will have you know," said Knightley, stubbornly, "I have a refined sense of humor."

Jake rolled his eyes and went to direct his friends in.

"I, for one, appreciate your sense of humor, Mr. Knightley," said JJ, a broad smile crossing his face.

"Kiss up," Jake said under his breath, glaring at him.

"No, just smart, "JJ said. "Anyway, I like him already."

"Nah," GG said as he slid into the room, "you're just a kiss up."

"Well, how would you like to proceed? Jake, offer these fine fellows something to eat—" suddenly, he stopped short.

"Who is this?" Knightley asked. He was shocked he had never picked the echolocation of the miniature mouse.

"Hello, my name is Moby. I am originally from Minnesota and was put in a shelter with parrots by accident. I think. When I was a baby. I am a Great Plains Pocket Mouse."

The three mice froze. Knightley flipped over again. The tiny mouse stood directly behind JJ, GG, and Jake.

"Like the whale?" Knightley asked. He gazed intently at the little mouse.

"What whale?" They all asked.

Knightley heaved a sigh.

"There is a famous book about a whale called Moby Dick. The family has memorized it, and—" Knightly was interrupted by a very serious Jake.

"Not the time," Jake said.

"Tell them how you got here," GG said. At last, Moby's story would be told! Maybe it would take a flyer to get him to speak.

"I came in the pocket of the man who came yesterday. That man works with Alpha."

"Alpha? Are you afraid of him?" asked Knightley.

"Oh no! He is wonderful!" Moby said. "I just know he is the father of the family here. I just had to find another thing to call him than 'owner'. I should have said father of this house. I still think of my owner as the man who came with me. My owner loves the owner who lives here! And even though my owner did that to the other mice, you know the story he told JJ and GG about tying the mice by their tails to the branch? Well, that was a long time ago. Now he takes care of animals. He does not know about me. There are a lot of birds in his house," he looked down, embarrassed.

The mice as one stiffened.

"Birds?" whispered GG.

"They are nice, mostly," Moby continued softly.

"What do you mean, 'mostly?'" JJ asked, stepping closer to Moby.

"Did you know that I met the girls from this house?" Moby said.

"What?" shouted Jake.

Moby moved backward.

"They came to my house, and they met Toby—" Moby started.

"Toby? The parrot who talked said, 'Hi, I'm Toby. What's your name?'" A very nervous Moby tried to clarify.

"To our girls?" Now JJ and GG were both shouting (they could not help but feel partially part of the human family and did not like that they would be loved by another house's animals. Don't forget, they came from a dynasty that passed down the family stories, and the girls had always loved them!).

"And you are Moby, named after the parrot Toby?" asked Knightley.

"Yes," Moby whispered. "The lady of my old house took me in. When they would call the bird 'Toby,' I thought Moby would be good enough because I am a mouse, so an

'M' would be a logical letter to start my name. The girls were so nice when they came. And one of them talked about how she did not mind mice living in her house. So, I intended to come whenever the opportunity made itself available because I always feared that the birds around me might find me and respond to their natural instincts. And then the master decided to come here. So, I did, too."

Knightley spanned out his wings. Moby began to retreat.

"It is very good you followed your instincts and left. Birds are a danger," Knightley stated.

Knightley's posture was relaxed now. This mouse had good instincts. They were logical. The fact that he listened to his logic and acted on it spoke well of him.

After the long, soft speech, the animals in the room were moved. Knightley's response also relieved the mice.

Jake was a little unnerved. If the Originals accepted him graciously, why would he not accept Moby, the newcomer, with equal graciousness? Besides, he was kind of adorable.

Jake promptly went over to Moby and clapped him on the back. Jake's well-intended greeting toppled the pocket mouse over.

"Oh, sorry!" Jake exclaimed as Moby righted himself.

"That's okay," Moby said.

Jake scampered out and came back with several bits of chocolate.

"The little sister keeps a store," he said in response to their questioning stares. "I thought dessert might be in order after our lovely dinner."

"Never could understand humans' attachment to sweets," said GG, his mouth full of chocolate.

"I could have cheese for dessert, too."

"Well, that hasn't stopped you, clearly," JJ said, eyeing the chocolate covering GG's fur.

Knightley cleared his throat meaningfully.

"Yes, well, we understand that you would like to offer your services in checking out the family's other home," said JJ, matter-of-factly.

Knightley flipped over, standing upright.

"Indeed. You are a bold, young rodent. Your forthrightness deserves respect. Hence, I am standing, though my legs are weak and wounded," Knightley said, favoring his right leg.

Jake groaned in embarrassment. "Please, Knightley, cut the act."

"I am greatly honored, Mr. Knightley," said JJ, not so gently shoving Jake.

"I know that the other part of the family comes every Wednesday, and finding a way into their vehicle would offer a secure ride for Jake," Knightley explained.

"That's tomorrow," said GG.

Jake swallowed audibly. "So, I will go and report back Wednesday after next."

Chapter 11: The Other Home

Jake was scared and excited. What an adventure! Jake had forgotten how much he loved his first adventure!

He quietly and unobtrusively managed to hide beneath the seats of the large vehicle. It was noisy beyond measure. Kids crying, laughing, and chattering. Parents chiding and soothing. He burrowed in the carpet, trying to block as much sound as possible. It didn't work.

Soon enough, though it did not feel quick, the car slowed. His heart racing, he waited (for a long while; it took them almost as much time to get out as it did to drive over). When they all cleared out, he flattened himself and eased out. He could see the house looming in front of him. Jake took a deep breath.

"Alright, here we go," he said. He tore off down the path. It was inky black. No shining lights across the field, barely any trees to gentle the terrain, not even the random headlights of a passing car. It was silent.

His heart was pounding so hard he was surprised it did not shoot out of his chest or echo in the dark, empty fields. He finally reached the door of the house.

His heart began to slow its frenzied pace.

"Alright," he said, drawing a calming breath. A smile began to form on his face. "I did it!"

"Not quite so fast," said a hissing, threatening voice from behind him. "You're not from around here, but I know where you're from. And now you are on my land. With my family. You should consider yourself dead."

Chapter 12: Tolkien's Warning

Tolkien was out of his mind with worry.

"These dumb mice! Aren't animals supposed to understand each other?!"

He was barking and growling and crying, and the only one paying him any mind was the woman who fed him until he was going to have a heart attack, only so she could keep him at bay.

"I wish I could find a way to tell her that I understand her," he said as she dumped yet another pile of dog food in front of him, "I leave her alone because she is freaked about everything. Plus, I owe her for mouthing her child. Even though I was gentle."

But he remembered when she told him, her always loving self, that she did not know whether to forgive him and if she could shoot him, she would, for biting her baby. He was genuinely chagrined.

As a last resort, he let out a piercing howl that could have brought down an owl. Finally, he heard scampering.

"What on earth!" exclaimed JJ. "What is wrong, Tolkien?"

And then he said the words that froze JJ's blood and would start the Clement Valley Mice and animals on a deadly adventure.

"They have a cat!"

Chapter 13: Sunny

The cat began circling the petrified Jake. He stood trembling, his mind running a thousand miles a minute.

Can this be it? That's it? he thought in disbelief and alarm.

She began to sniff Jake.

"You smell like the kids when they come from the Other Place," she said, her voice dripping disdain.

"Horses and goats and sheep, filth! And then mice, oh, so many mice," she purred.

"But we don't have mice here," she continued, laying across the doorstep. "Oh no, we have no mice. And my family is proud of that. And everyone loves me. They come out just to see me."

Jake began thinking of ways to escape. Distract her? No. That would not work. What is her plan?

She began to laugh, not nicely. She stood again.

"What? Cat got your tongue," she said. She slapped him with her paw.

"That is a very inappropriate attempt at humor," said Jake as he stood trembling, trying to say exactly what he thought Knightley would say.

She stopped the threatening growl she was using to intimidate him.

"Well, well, an articulate little upstart," she said in mild surprise.

Suddenly there was a noise from inside. Someone opened the door with a crack and stuck their head out.

"Sunny? Are you okay?"

Sunny covered her new plaything and began to purr, but this purr was different. Soft and gentle.

"They think you are sweet and lovable. But you sound nauseating!" Jake's voice was muffled beneath her paw. He figured this was the safest time to get 'catty' with her while she was forced to play lovable in front of her people.

The house owner went back inside. Sunny eased away from Jake, placing her paw on his tail.

"Clearly, they don't call you Sunny for your disposition. They should call you Evil. And Conniving."

A mouse's tail is not only his balance but his dignity. Sunny knew this.

"Yes, well," she said, grinning wickedly, "to each his own. I love my people and am very nice to them, even when they pull my tail. But I hate mice. And dogs. And, oh, well, one of my family's humans."

She let out a little growl mentioning the human she hated.

"I tried to go and be affectionate with her," she said, her voice bitter, "and she told me that she does not like me and not to love her or even go anywhere near her!"

Jake bristled. He recollected a conversation the one they loved had with her sister about how she was allergic to cats and hated that when she went to her brother's house, their cat kept coming up to her and rubbing against her legs.

"She's just allergic," he said, his posture becoming rigid and defensive.

"Whatever. She is not on my good side. And neither are you. Not just because you came to her defense for no good reason."

Jake garnered the courage to ask a dreaded question.

"Why don't you just kill me and be over with it?"

She began to laugh softly, evilly.

"Good question, my over-educated mouse. Because I need you to do something for me."

Chapter 14: Disaster

JJ stood, almost frozen on the spot, if not for his twitching tail.

"Cat?" he whispered.

A minute later, GG came running up. Catching his petrified cousin's last word, 'cat', he shrieked, looking around wildly.

"Where?!"

"GG!" JJ took his near hysterical cousin by the shoulders. "Just calm down so we can think straight."

"'Thinking straight' won't save Jake!" GG felt that calming down was wrong.

"Oh, but for some reason, you think being hysterical will? Can you hear what you are saying?" JJ reasoned with his cousin.

Tolkien looked between the two mice.

"I don't know what to tell you," the concerned dog said, sitting down, "but I think the sooner someone goes over to bring him back, the better."

JJ and GG looked at each other and then back at Tolkien.

"You are Tolkien!" came a tentative yet oddly confident squeak.

The whites of Tolkien's eyes began to show. He emitted a low sound. It was not quite a growl but a fearful sound of the unknown.

GG and JJ stood close to Moby.

"What are you doing?" asked JJ. His tail was waving side to side. "Why didn't you allow us to introduce you? And now is not the time, Moby!"

"He is nice to you guys. Why should he be different with me?" Moby asked.

"He has a good point, you know." Tolkien watched the little mouse thoughtfully. "But who are you?"

"I'm Moby," when Tolkien started to respond, he continued, "and, no, not like the whale."

I have to read this story, thought Moby.

"Thank you for the answer, and now there is no time for introductions," said Tolkien.

"Well," said JJ tentatively, once the awkward interruption finished, "you have been there, right?"

Tolkien stood up abruptly, startling the mice.

GG said excitedly, "You can save him!"

Tolkien barked in frustration.

"You know I cannot go by myself!"

GG placed himself behind JJ before he said, "That's not true. You do go places by yourself when you want to. Nobody will miss you in the morning."

He began to growl.

JJ started to back away.

"Now, Tolkien," he began, "that was just an idea. No one is going to force you."

"As if we could," muttered GG under his breath.

"Listen, I cannot go on my own. My boy would be worried out of his mind."

"You have a boy? I know him! Or of him. My old master wouldn't let him come over—"

A low rumble began in Tolkien's throat. "What do you mean he wouldn't let him go over? He is the best boy in the world!"

The mice inched closer to one another.

"For sure, that very nice man had nothing against your boy, Tolkien. He is friends with the father of the house and would never not love his son!" said GG. Tolkien registered that and sat down. GG was right. Tolkien would not have to tear him apart after all.

"Alright, alright," said JJ, placatingly, "now that we are done with that intense introduction, can you just tell us what happens when you do go?"

Tolkien smiled and sat back down.

"Sunny is terrified when I am around," he said blissfully. "She usually tries to get in the house, and when they don't let her in, she runs up a tree."

The mice gawked in amazement. He could really protect Jake! They were more determined than ever to get him there.

"Well, thank you for the warning, Tolkien," JJ said, darting off with GG and Moby right behind him.

"What are you doing, JJ?" GG asked as they slipped into their enclave.

"I can always tell when you have a plan," GG continued.

"A plan? Tell me! I'll help," Moby said.

"It's not that big of a plan, Pipsqueak," said JJ, "We just have to talk to Knightley."

He strode off rapidly, a mouse with a plan.

"We have to take something up for him, not just out of respect, but I am sure he is hungry," said JJ thoughtfully.

"Well, there is some cheese," said GG.

"I am pretty sure he is a fruit bat," JJ responded.

"Then bananas." GG was irritated with what he considered to be excessive protocol.

"I would think grapes would be a better offer," Moby said.

"Oh, come on, GG," said JJ, exasperated, "if for nothing else, the guy's gotta eat!"

"Alright, alright," said GG, running off to the kitchen.

He stored a hefty bite of cheese in the pouch of his mouth and dashed back to JJ. Together, the three clawed their way up the rocks and followed the previous path into Knightley's closet.

"Mr. Knightley," JJ whispered as they quietly walked into the closet.

They caught sight of the bat, camouflaged in a dark garment at the very corner of the closet.

Knightley opened one eye.

"Have you any idea what time it is?" he droned.

The mice were nervous but determined.

"We are so very sorry, Mr. Knightley—" JJ, trying to maintain his respectfully cautious demeanor, began to say.

"But we brought you food!" GG interrupted, anxious to appease the disgruntled bat.

"And we figured," he continued, further angering the bat in his attempt to appease him, "that you would still be awake, considering the people are still all asleep."

JJ simply shut his eyes, pretending this was not happening.

The bat opened both eyes and looked at the mice.

"Well," he said, "what is so important, besides the food, which I thank you for, that you had to wake me in the middle of the morning?"

GG removed a banana from his mouth, handing it over to the bat.

"There you go," he said, trying to smile. GG did not quite succeed.

"Mr. Knightley," said JJ, clearing his throat, "Tolkien just told us there is a cat at the house Jake just went to."

Mr. Knightley flipped onto his legs in alarm. In his agitation, he left the closet.

"Oh no!" he exclaimed, gliding around the room. "My poor boy!"

JJ, GG, and Moby watched, uncertain how to react to a flying bat at such close quarters.

"Yes, he is definitely in danger, and we have to save him," said GG, following the circling bat with his eyes. "And we thought to ask you if you have any ideas about how to."

"We were wondering, more precisely, if you could help us find a way to get Tolkien to the other house," JJ said, "because the cat is afraid of him, and that would free Jake if..."

Knightley silently swooped down into the closet. He settled on the bar. When he spoke, his voice betrayed his anxiety.

"I cannot begin to express mys—" his voice broke, and he began to clear his throat, "I am clearly upset and cannot gather my thoughts."

"You really do love him!" Moby said. Not willing to be left behind, he followed JJ and GG as fast as his little legs could take him.

So, flyers really can care about us! But this house does have a strange effect on animals, so that does not mean it is normal. Or that Toby would love me. With that thought, Moby stopped his meandering mind.

The cousins looked down, uncertain of how to react and even of how to feel. For Mr. Knightley — whom they came to seeking a solution for a terrifying dilemma — to have this reaction upset their fragile balance of determination and courage.

"No," said GG, his tone of voice displaying unusual confidence, "Mr. Knightley, I do not believe that you, of all creatures, with your years and years of experience and your batliness that allows you to see things from a perspective that the, what did you call us, yeah, earthbound creatures, cannot see, 'cannot gather your thoughts'."

The bat flipped over the bar and stood on his legs, looking at GG.

"Well said, cuz! And so true!" said JJ, patting his cousin on the back.

"Flyers do have a lot of vision! Mr. Knightley is more influential than even Toby!" Moby said. To know that a creature could best Toby the parrot satisfied him immensely.

"Thank you, GG and Moby," began Knightley, looking seriously at GG (usually, it was JJ who was awarded that kind of attention). "Your surprising vote of confidence, and a reminder of my general aptitude for capabilities of the mind, was encouraging."

JJ did not know whether he should simply feel happy that Knightley was coming back to a rational state of mind or overwhelmingly irritated with the bat's massive ego.

"Now that we have established that you are very smart, how are your mind's capabilities going to find a way to save Jake?" JJ managed to say this with minimal annoyance.

"That's rude," said GG, his newfound confidence finding a voice.

"Listen, one good speech does not give you license to start throwing around opinions," JJ snapped, angry that he was rightly chastised.

"Hey, I was right, and you know it!" GG said.

"Stop!" Knightley ordered, "I heard The Owner's planning to leave in two days' time, which will give Tolkien a golden opportunity to travel to the other house."

"A lot can happen in two days," said JJ quietly.

"Which is why I will fly there, after you take me to Tolkien, so he can give me precise directions," Knightley said.

"But," said JJ, almost as though he were thinking aloud, "are you able to fly the distance with your damaged wing?"

The bat gathered his wings to his body. After a moment, he lifted his head, looking straight at the expectant trio of mice.

"The circumstances do not allow for failure," he said, sparks of determination nearly shooting out of his eyes.

Chapter 15: Jake and Sunny

"Something for you?" Jake asked, trying to discreetly remove his tail from under her paw.

"Yes, and stop trying to move your tail. You never will be able to," Sunny stated matter-of-factly.

Jake surrendered for a moment but fully intended on continuing any escape plan when an opportunity provided itself.

"Fine. What do you want from me that only I can give you?" the mouse asked, a hint of sarcasm in his voice.

"Oh, you know it is not only you," the cat said, unphased, "you are just here, alone and vulnerable. It is much funner when the prey can be immobilized from all angles."

Her silky, smooth voice and scent were beginning to overwhelm him. His ability to ignore her pervasive cat smell and the sound of her voice was being tested.

"That is evil, to hurt creatures and enjoy it!" Jake said as emphatically as he could while being trapped.

She just smiled, her tail lazily swishing.

"I need you to get me in the house, so I can lay on the soft bed in the guest room. If the mother sees you running around in her home, she will almost certainly bring me in."

"So, that's my point?" he asked, his mind beginning to run with ideas of escape once he got in.

Sunny deftly unsheathed her claws above his tail.

"Do not think of getting ideas of escape," she hissed.

Jake's heart began to race, feeling the sharpness of the claws. If she just swiped one, his tale would be sliced.

"I understand," Jake said. His voice was subdued, his spirits even more so.

Near tears, he thought, *Oh, Knightley, where are you?*

Chapter 16: The Bat and the Mice

The mice kindly guided Knightley down by way of the stairs. They jumped swiftly down the stairs while the bat glided smoothly above them.

"I do not need your direction in a house that I know very well!" Knightley was frustrated with what he perceived to be coddling.

"You can only know it so well because of your' echo system' that has this house mapped out for you," said JJ as he made the final jump to the ground floor.

"Repeating back my words to me, which, by the way, are very true, is almost rude!" declared Knightley.

"You can't blame us for being worried. It's not that we don't believe you," said GG, his tone soothing, "we just want to make sure that when Jake gets back, he won't kill us for leaving you alone."

"I am not an invalid!" Knightley finally hollered.

GG looked away, uncomfortable with the bat's uncharacteristic emotional expression.

"That is debatable," JJ said under his breath.

Knightley took a deep breath, gathering himself.

"First, let me extend my apologies for my outburst of emotion. I understand that not only has my wing been torn a bit, and my leg was previously broken, but," he said, raising his hand to silence the mice's reaction, "sometimes one has to weigh the balance and determine when overexertion of one's abilities is called for."

The bat waited silently for his words to sink in. He saw when the mice registered what he meant. He could tell when they very badly wanted to object, but they could not when they saw the validity of his claim.

"Yeah," said GG with a sniffle, "I see what you mean."

"It is very noble of you, Mr. Knightley," JJ said.

"It is normal for emotions to overspill when the stakes and tensions are high, and we are certainly embarking on an abnormal journey, but please, inform Tolkien of my presence," Knightley stated, back to business.

"That is so beautiful," Moby said. His eyes looked like saucers on his small face. He clearly was deeply moved.

JJ collapsed his bone structure and eased through a hole in the bottom of the door.

"Tolkien," JJ whispered, seeing the dog in his usual place in front of the house door. "The bat is here on the other side of this door."

Tolkien bounded up, startled and disgruntled.

"The bat!?" he asked, confused. "What bat? And what has that got to do with me?" At this point, a low growl was beginning to reach his throat.

"Tolkien!" shouted JJ, "Would you please not do that! It frays every one of my nerves, and we are on the same side!"

"I know, sorry," said Tolkien, resuming a seated position, "but I have never dealt with a flying creature–"

"Not true," JJ interrupted, "remember the chickens?"

"Yeah, that is true, but I never dealt with a flying mouse!" he exclaimed.

"I would not tell that to him. He considers himself several thousand steps above, well, all creatures," JJ said wryly. "In any case, he just wants directions to get to the other house so he can help Jake until you go in a few days."

"What?" he barked, jumping up again, "I told you I could not go because of my master!"

"My goodness, would you stop barking and sit down?" JJ pleaded with him, "the whole family is leaving in two days, so you can go and bring the bat and Jake back."

"Hmph," Tolkien huffed. "Fine, send him out."

JJ darted through door hole. He saw GG and Knightley waiting, hardly visible in the corner of the bookcase next to the door.

"Okay, he's ready, Mr. Knightley," JJ informed Knightley.

"Are we sure about this, guys?" asked GG nervously.

"As we'll ever be," JJ said solemnly. *This could be a disaster,* he thought to himself.

The bat, without a word, flitted through the hole and into Tolkien's place.

"What?" shouted GG, "He doesn't say anything? Just zip through the door, and that's it!?"

Chapter 17: The Bat and the Dog

"Well," said Knightley, "finally, we meet, and you are not simply an echo."

He studied Tolkien. He was surprisingly dignified looking, though a bit grungy. *Much to offer if he would just listen to me,* he mused.

For some odd reason, Tolkien felt compelled to stand and straighten himself upon the sight of the bat. *This is no mouse, flying or otherwise. I think I like him.*

"And you are not just an echolocation," Tolkien responded, sitting, so as not to take an intimidating stance in front of the smaller creature.

"I have come, my canine friend, to get directions to the other house," the bat informed him.

Tolkien looked at Knightley for a moment before saying, "Are you certain you can fly?"

The bat looked away and said, "If I fly in the direction the wind is blowing, it can take a great deal of pressure off my wings, and I can glide easily."

Tolkien nodded, saying, "It is a good thing that the south easterly winds will guide you through the northwestern airway."

"Yes, indeed," pleasantly surprised by the dog's attention to detail, "I always knew you were more than meets the eye."

Tolkien was caught between pleasure at the compliment and the urge to snap his teeth—a very intimidating canine response—at the underlying insult. *No matter,* he thought, *I'll show him.*

"You will head northwest when you fly out of the house here. Per normal bat flying patterns, you should drop from the northwest corner of the balcony. That is your point of origin. Your velocity will be determined depending on your acceleration level while falling and barring any displacement due to unanticipated wind changes. You should hover, letting the wind do most of the work. You have roughly six miles to fly, and to the best of your abilities, to conserve your energy, remember you will still have to be cunning with Sunny, the cat.

"You will fly first over the forest. Then you will cross over fields, then Pine Creek. There, you may want to take a drink of water to boost your energy level, which is only a minor displacement. It will continue to be mostly fields, with some other small reservoirs. When you pass over a pasture with cows, you will fly over a cornfield and then reach the bales of hay. They are a house with a blue roof. And the only visible house."

Well, well, the bat thought, *though I knew there was more than meets the eye, I seriously underestimated how much more there was than meets the eye.*

"Clearly," began Knightley, "I have offended you. You are letting me know by way of displaying your knowledge of kinematics. I am sorry for the offense but understand, I was actually complimenting you. But you are surprisingly scientifically eloquent. In comparison to most creatures."

Tolkien's initial discomfort was alleviated.

"I believe it is true that cats are very... well uncomfortable with bats. Are you depending on that?" Tolkien asked.

"Well," said the bat smiling, "I will never fully depend on anything, but, yes, I am counting on that holding me over until you arrive."

"Okay, now that that is clear, I would advise you to use the upstairs balcony as your starting position due to the southwest blowing wind and the simplicity of the directions from that angle," said Tolkien.

"That seems sound," said Knightley, smiling. Climbing
the door to fit in through the hole, he turned and said, "thank
you kindly, my dear friend."

Chapter 18: The Rescue Begins

The mice were worried. JJ was pacing back and forth in their little enclave in front of the door. GG tapped his little paw repeatedly. Moby sat in the farthest corner, still and silent.

JJ abruptly stopped walking.

"How come we are not hearing anything?" said JJ.

GG stopped tapping long enough to say, "JJ, we just guided him down here four minutes ago!"

There was a slight sound of fluttering. The mice jumped up expectantly.

"My dear mice," Knightley began, "we have a plan–"

"We?" asked GG, "When did we make it?"

The bat laughed, "No, no, Tolkien and me."

The mice stared at him, open-mouthed.

"You and Tolkien?" JJ asked, puzzled.

"Wait," he continued, "You liked him!"

"Well, yes, I did indeed. You have severely misrepresented him. He is quite brilliant, in fact."

Now the mice were dumbfounded.

"Tolkien?" GG repeated, "Brilliant?"

He looked at JJ and began to laugh. Moby looked at the bat curiously.

"No, he can't be. He is just lazy," GG said.

JJ was watching the bat closely.

"No," he murmured, "Knightley would not say that unless there is truth to it, so shut up, GG."

"Now, my friends, it is understandable that Tolkien would not find a reason to show his genius mind to you. He only did it with me because he was giving me detailed instructions on how to save your kin. We should go back upstairs to the balcony where you can send me off."

The mice were only mildly placated.

"I think you should ask your genius new friend to take you upstairs," GG said bitterly. "GG, knock it off," JJ reprimanded GG, "we have a friend in distress, and if Tolkien can help – who we went to for help – if you remember, then he is doing what we went to him for."

"That's true!" said GG, brightening up, "so it *is* because of us in the end!"

"Whatever makes you feel better," said JJ.

"I think you guys should try to hide your massive insecurity. I can only imagine what you would be like with

Toby," Moby said. The cousins stared him down. Moby proved to be not so easily intimidated.

"Lead the way, my little friends!" said Knightley, flying up the staircase silently above the scampering mice.

They reached the landing and made a left. Crossing the table (GG saw a couple of lone crumbs and stooped to pick them up), they zipped under the door that opened up to the balcony.

"We never come here," said GG, nervously eyeing the vastness of open air.

"Hardly ever. Anyhow, it is far too open and not quite safe." JJ added.

The bat took in the view. Remembering Tolkien's directions, he looked over the forested area he would fly over. His main concern was the unwanted presence of owls, and he could see the pine tree cavity, which most certainly an owl used as a resting space.

"You are correct in not venturing out here," his ears picking up the echoes of multiple dangers.

"Mr. Knightley," began JJ, "you must be careful. I am sure there are a lot of dangers for you, too."

"Do not forget, my friends," said the bat, positioning himself on the railing, "that it is daylight, and my main predators are sleeping now."

"Who are they?" asked Moby, his eyes wide with fear.

"Owls," Knightley responded shortly before dropping from the ledge and spreading his wings.

GG let out a screech of terror at the mention of 'owls' and shot into the house. JJ and Moby were not far behind him.

"Listen, GG," JJ said calmly, though the mention of 'owl' did jolt him a bit, "you have to be calm. In all of our years — no, decades here — no owl has ever managed to get in. And they do not have a sense of smell. And we never leave."

"You are just as nervous, JJ," said GG as they jumped down the rocks, "so don't act all collected."

"That is true," said JJ, "but I didn't shriek and run. I just calmly went back in."

"Again…" Moby started.

"Don't say it, Whaley!" GG said, interrupting Moby, "We know we would not know what to do with Toby."

Rolling his eyes, JJ seated himself on the hay in their crevice.

"Here," he said, offering his cousin and Moby breadcrumbs.

They sat quietly, enjoying their bread and trying to shake off their anxiety.

"Now what?" asked GG.

"We wait."

"That's it?"

"Well, yeah," JJ responded, staunchly not meeting GG's gaze, "I mean, what else can we do?"

"We did a good job, right, JJ?" asked GG.

JJ looked up, his eyes filled with concern for his cousin, worry for Moby in his new surroundings, anxiety about the bat's trip, terror for Jake, and overwhelming exhaustion.

"Yeah, we did. We did all we could anyway," he said, patting GG on the back, "and now the best thing we can do is sleep, so we can be ready for their return. All of them."

Chapter 19: Bird's Eye View

Tolkien strained his ears, trying to hear the progress of the bat. He listened to the pitter-patter of the mice, the squeaking of the balcony floorboards, and then not too long after, the drop and take off the bat.

They are daring, those mice, to come out to the open, he told himself. *They are noble little creatures. Knightley is dignified as well. He, if anyone, deserves their nobility.* He settled into a comfortable lying position. *We will see what happens soon,* he thought, drifting to sleep.

Knightley heard the breathing of Tolkien, his surprising new companion, standing with his paws on the doorstep. He could almost hear him listening for the bat's movements. He heard the dog turn around and stretch out to sleep. *He will be fine,* thought the bat. *I only hope he can save myself and my protégé soon.*

Knightley was indeed ready to brave any and all dangers for his protégé and well aware of the risks that could await him. They would start with the birds at the feeders. Though they would be wary of him as he was a bat and a predator, their fear could make them aggressive. He had to lower his ultrasonic pulses that other creatures normally could detect. But there was another problem he could not ignore. It was broad daylight even if he was not signaling to other creatures. As soon as he started gliding above the birds, they started incessant chatter amongst themselves concerning his strangeness; commenting that he probably had rabies and was crazy, and it took every bit of his control to not heighten his pulsating sounds to make them filled with fear. No, he would never lower himself in that fashion! He was on a mission, and they probably could never understand as they were most likely very uneducated!

He determined to stay above the streets and steer clear of forested areas. He did have to skim over the water reservoir to replenish his water. Luckily, the tadpoles were too small and too terrified of him to be a worry, and their parents were nowhere to be seen.

So, six miles and two hours later, Knightley saw a metallic blue roof and set off amid a gently rolling pasture. Peaceful and unobtrusive, it was different from the other house. The surrounding forest of his home was a source of never-ending chatter. The noisy daylight animals quietly turned into the stealthy hunting sounds of the night-time critters.

The bat could see the charm of this place for a cat. An impenetrable silence filled the area, indicating that all the living creatures were hiding from something: Sunny.

She was the unchallenged queen of this kingdom, making his mission all the more difficult.

Knightley rose above the tree line, distancing himself from the cat's sight and smell range. His ultrasonic pulses were barely detectable, so the other creatures would be mostly unaware. He moved forward, hovering above the sparsely populated trees. He listened to the surrounding echoes. Tons of bugs. Birds. Rabbits. Frogs. Possum. And a woman screaming. He knew that scream. In his house, that woman used to live there, and she was not fond of mice. Or bats, for that matter. That could only mean one thing. Jake was inside.

Chapter 20: Inside Out

"Now, I am going to remove my paw," said Sunny, "and you will go inside."

Jake was trembling. Overwhelmed by being trapped by a cat, by being out in the open, in a place he had no knowledge of, and then by a particular scent that wafted across his nose. His heart soared.

Knightley! he thought. *I cannot believe it, that crazy bat. I am sure this is not good for him!*

His heart began to race, fearing that Sunny would smell his loyal friend and react. His one hope was that Knightley would be a foreign smell to the cat, and she might not pick up on the connection between her captive and the bat. Bats made cats uncomfortable.

But all of those reasons would only hold for a while. His mind was racing with ideas.

"So," started Jake, "you're going to let go of my tail, and I just go in. And then what?"

She began to softly graze one claw over his tail.

"You don't trust me?" she asked, laughing. "Good, you are getting smart."

"I am a mouse," said Jake, beginning to sweat, "we are programmed to mistrust you. And you are using that to your advantage."

"Yes, yes," she agreed, complacent in her power, "I am, aren't I?"

Jake had to play his cards correctly now. He was terrified, so he did not have to act that part. What he had to cover was his elation. She knew he would be happy to be away from her, but she did not know about his sense of hope. Sunny would anticipate his eagerness to be away, but she had threatened him enough to believe him hopeless.

Jake scowled at her.

"You disgust me," he said passionately. He understood that a display of despair portrays a creature's vulnerability.

"Oh," Sunny said mockingly, "how sad for you. Now, go on in. And do not forget, I will know if you try to escape me."

She lifted her paw, liberating him. Though he shot out faster than a bullet, Jake's heart was filled with the fear of her threat. He had to find Knightley. When he was out of Sunny's line of sight, he stopped moving and began to smell. His nose was accosted by a million new smells. The house was filled with light, very different than his home, shaded by forest. The house smelled mostly of cat.

"Of course, there would be no mice, or any vermin for that matter, with that beast!" he muttered. The door opened, and two things happened: One, he caught a whiff of Knightley, and two, he wasn't allowed to revel in the nearness of the bat because the woman started to scream.

Chapter 21: The Plan Begins to Unfold

Knightley folded his wings on the upstroke despite the dull ache. As he ceased flapping them and coasted the wind, the discomfort began to subside.

"Now, my young sportsman, I will just be a moment," he told Jake in the empty air.

The house was coming close into view. There were many windows and three doors. The echolocation placed Jake downstairs. *Somewhere with a bathroom,* he thought, *and a gutter with a window.*

He veered to the left, where he could hear the bathroom plumbing. The window was at the top of the gutter. He maneuvered himself to sink down to the little opening that caught his eye. Collapsing his bones and sliding through the space, he succeeded in flying into the room.

There was a bed beneath him, and the door to the bathroom was roughly six feet away. He floated into the bathroom. There was the mouse! Jake looked up at his friend, his eyes filled with relief and amazement.

"I can't believe it," he whispered. "I am so glad to see you, Knightley."

"Hush, now," said Knightley, relief pouring through him at the sight of his young companion, "You couldn't imagine me doing anything less miraculous now, could you, due to my vast experience and capabilities?"

Jake began to laugh, overwhelmed by an intense wave of emotion. "I am so glad to know you haven't changed much, Knightley. But tell me how you knew?"

"Well," began Knightley, "that is mostly due to GG, JJ, Moby, and even Tolkien, who is, by the way, greatly misunderstood."

Jake was stunned when Knightley told him the course of events.

"That is amazing!" he exclaimed, "I don't know which part is most surprising, the mice or smarty pants Tolkien."

"Now is not the time to analyze the wonders of our household animal bondings," Knightley said,

"We need to discuss our plan of escape."

Jake was jolted out of his state of tenderness for his loyal companion and newfound friends. "Sunny will know!" he said, beginning to shiver.

Knightley could see genuine fear in Jake's eyes.

"Tell me, my friend, what transpired between you and the cat?"

The mouse described the cat's capture and her deal with him.

"So, now," he finished, "I have to keep the woman's attention until she lets the cat in."

Knightley, hanging upside down with his eyes closed, flipped over. Standing straight up, he said, "We have been cloistered long enough, and you have some terrifying to do, so run out, and terrorize the household's mistress enough to have the cat sent in."

"Knightley!" cried out Jake, "What are you saying?"

"Jake, stop panicking, and start thinking!" Knightley said. "We have to get through this time."

Knightley looked at the traumatized mouse.

"Allowing for the cat to come in is part of saving us," he held up his hand to stop Jake from talking.

"And when she comes in," Despite Knightley's level tone of voice, Jake could have sworn there was a vengeful gleam in his eyes, "I will introduce myself to her."

"Knightley," Jake said, looking at Knightley directly, "what are you up to?"

"Absolutely nothing. Other than utilizing the natural apprehension cats feel with bats to my advantage."

Jake laughed, "Well, there's a threat if I ever heard one!"

"Well," said Knightley, his voice deceptively monotone as he stretched his wings, "it is the very least she deserves. After all she put you through."

Jake looked fondly at his savior before saluting Knightley and jumping lightly off the ledge.

"Alright, time to complete *Operation Get Cat In*," Jake paused before saying, "and get back at her!"

Chapter 22: The Cat in the House

Sunny did not think of herself as particularly mean. She actually thought she was rather nice.

Oh, she knew cats had a reputation of aloofness, but she thought of herself more as puppy-like. Though she hated that comparison, that is what the owners always said. They said it fondly, so she imitated dogs as much as she could without demeaning the natural superiority of cats.

She busied herself by grooming and contemplating the patheticness dogs represented. If only she did not fear them so much. She hated running and hiding.

At least she could run and hide from them, she thought, *not like bats. Ah, those bane of mammal-kind.* They were few and far between here, in her home, but she remembered her old haunt with a shudder. They were so quiet. Not quite so quiet as owls—now those birds terrified her—but bats were quiet enough to sneak up on her. They kept to themselves mostly, but they were elite among forest creatures and made felines look like mice. They made her, well, uneasy.

"What is that mouse doing? It has been too long…" she was cut off when the door flew open, and the mistress came running out.

"Sunny! Please come in and get that mouse!!"

The cat sat up straight and charged into the house.

"Mouse!" Sunny hissed, "Come out of hiding."

Sunny hunkered down, her tail swishing, her nose to the ground. She began to ease forward, stalking her prey.

"Come now, don't be scared. You are following instructions nicely," she purred. All of a sudden, she straightened. She felt a nearly imperceptible shift in the air.

"Oh, hello," came a deep-voiced greeting.

Sunny meowed. Her voice betrayed her apprehension.

"No," said Knightley, his voice icy, silently gliding above her, extending his wings to intimidate, "this will certainly not do."

"How strange," the cat said sharply, nervously looking up, trying to keep the bat in sight, "if I didn't know better, I would think you are being protective."

"Ah," said Knightley, as though he were pontificating. "I suppose it is good that I can tell you, with utmost authority, that you know nothing in the first place to know anything enough to know 'better'."

A low purr began to resonate in her voice as she walked around, her fear level rising under the shade of his wings.

"What do you want?"

"Well," Knightley began, "first, tell me what you did to my friend."

The cat decided on another tact and stretched out across the floor.

"I was just teasing him," she said, rolling over and lying on her back, "he's a mouse, for heaven's sake. That's what we cats do with mice."

The bat began to sing at a chirp level, revealing his strength only the cat could hear.

And she did. She stood up, hissing.

"Stop it!" she growled.

The bat laughed.

"Did you think I would not understand your outwardly aggressive stance of lying down on your back? I am unlike your human caretakers, who would mistake that seemingly passive position as compliance."

Sunny snarled at Knightley, her ears pointed straight up. She sprung up on her haunches.

"What do you want?" she growled.

Knightley hovered just above the cat's reach and decided that he had paid the cat back enough for tormenting his little ward.

"Well, now that you have tasted some of what you put the poor mouse through—and be aware that it is not nearly comparable to the torture Jake went through—I will lighten my well-orchestrated vengeance."

He settled lightly on one of the pipes in the ceiling of the large, windowed room.

"You have two things that have saved you from my wrath," said Knightley. "One, you did not kill Jake, and two, the kids love you."

Sunny calmed down and rearranged herself into a comfortable position. The bat meant no harm.

"Explain to me," she said, in an aloof tone, "what this odd relationship with you and that mouse is, exactly."

Knightley assessed the cat using his years of experience. He did not exaggerate when he gave his reasons for how she was not a threat. True, she was a cat, with all the foibles and natural instincts her nature gave her, but she did not seem to exploit her innate feline capacities.

"In response to your rather invasive question," Knightley still had to keep Sunny in her place despite his conclusion that, as far as cats went, she wasn't so bad, "Jake just happened to be outside the room the mistress of the other house was in when she had me removed. "

The bat remained silent. The cat paused her grooming to prod him.

"Yes…" she said, "do continue."

"Well, my fair lady, when I flew out, I startled a mother squirrel. She lashed out at me, breaking my already weak leg and tearing my wing. Jake happened to be there when I fell. He guided me through a hole in the wall, where we took up residence in one of the closets after a few treacherous days with a mother bird. He shed his skin a bit and wrapped my leg with the excess skin. And he brings me food as well."

"He wrapped your leg with his skin? That is appalling," said Sunny, shuddering in disgust.

"Not so, my prejudiced feline. A mouse's fur has infection preventive properties," Knightley said, his voice laden with satisfaction for being able to vouch for mice to a cat.

Sunny purred in mild irritation.

"You don't have to be so self-satisfied, trying to prove mice to me," she unfurled from her lackadaisical position, "you'll never convince me."

Now Knightley was irritated. He began to hum. Sunny immediately fell out of her overly relaxed grooming and meowed in agitation.

"Stop it!" she hissed, "You should be above cheap vengeance!"

Knightley stopped and began chuckling in satisfaction.

"Ahh," he said, "There are few things more satisfying than vexing a cat."

"Now that you are done being petty, which does not suit you, by the way," said Sunny, "I assume you have a plan."

"We do," Knightley stated, not yet about to let the cat off the hook.

"Oh, come on now, bat! I am pretty sure that at some point, you are going to need me!" Sunny was frustrated (and still a little uneasy).

"Well, now that you mention it," Knightley said with an infuriating calm, "we do need you to run out to the house mistress carrying my little friend gently."

The cat began to groom herself, almost as if she had no care in the world.

"First, I would like to lie down on the bed in the room with the bathroom, down here, and then I will do as you ask."

"Fine," the bat responded, "but be well aware that I am dealing with you in a time of truce. Do not, for even a second, think to torment the mouse in any possible way."

The cat stiffened and began to purr beseechingly, "I can't even tease him a bit?"

"If by teasing him you mean unleashing your claws, or hissing, or making him feel imprisoned, or threatened, no, you cannot."

"Oh, you're such a stickler. It is almost unfair for you to make me behave in such an unnatural way," she grumbled.

"I am only asking that you take care to not put yourself in a… shall we say... dangerous position."

She hissed at Knightley as she went through the door and stalked to the bed. She laid herself languorously across the coveted bed.

This might make it worth it. A little nap in luxury does not happen all that much, she thought as her eyes drifted shut.

The bat silently flew into the room and saw her sleeping.

Not that I would trust that she is sleeping, but she is harmless. Possibly even good. It does mean a lot that she did not eat him. I think I can trust that she will even bring Jake to me safely, Knightley thought.

He set off to the room with the hanging pipes to inform his friend of the ensuing plan.

Chapter 23: Plan Executed

Jake darted directly into the woman's line of vision. Torn between fear of the woman, and terror of the cat, it was easy for him to find the nearest hiding spot. The woman tore out of the house, and Sunny quickly came charging in.

"Mouse," he heard her hiss, and his blood ran cold, "come out of hiding."

Knightley! Where are you? he thought in panic.

Soon enough, he heard, in a tone of voice that was absolutely terrifying, if he wasn't sure that it was not really directed towards him:

"Well, hello."

Knightley is as terrifying to that cat as she is to me! He thought. He watched, without being able to hear exactly what was going on, from his hiding spot as Knightley and Sunny played a nervewracking Bat and Mouse game, where he felt like he was the intended prize slash victim. It did not make him feel particularly nice. Soon enough, he saw Sunny saunter off to the room Knightley found Jake in.

"Jake," the bat called out, "you can come out now."

The mouse skittered out from under the shoe rack.

"Knightley, what are you doing?!" He exclaimed in alarm. "She is still here!"

"Not to worry, my friend," Knightley said placatingly, "she will do you no harm."

Jake stared at his friend in shock.

"What do you mean, 'she will do you no harm?' Are you out of your mind? She will do me every harm!"

"Now, now, Jake, you must have some faith in me. If I tell you that, you should trust that I know of what I speak."

Jake's muscles relaxed. A bit.

"Alright, old friend. Can you tell me exactly what is going on?"

The bat settled onto the shoe rack ledge. *Too low for me to hang down on. This is exceedingly uncomfortable,* he thought.

"Please prepare yourself to be alarmed, but do not respond until I am finished," the bat said.

Jake glared at him but was obediently quiet.

"My young friend, Sunny is…"

Jake straightened in a mix of fury and hurt.

"'Sunny'! What do you mean calling her 'Sunny', like she is an old friend?!"

"Calm yourself, Jake. I am not friends with the cat. I am simply calling her by her given name," Knightley responded with recalcitrant calm.

Jake curled himself up, saying petulantly,

"Sounds pretty friendly to me."

The bat flew off the ledge and settled next to Jake.

"Jake, do not jump to conclusions. With what I am asking her to do, she deserves to be called by her name."

The mouse sat up fearfully.

"Bat guy, I do not like the sound of this," he told Knightley.

"And I am sure you will hate what I will say now. The cat, following my instructions, will pick you up and show the owners where you are captured. They will think she will finish you off, but she will bring you to me."

At this point, the mouse was fidgeting in terror.

"Knightley, please no!"

"Now, now, do not worry," Knightley said comfortingly, "I promise, she will do nothing to harm you in any way. And Tolkien will come and take us home shortly after that."

Chapter 25: Tolkien's Trip

Tolkien, the future hero, was at that moment running around the house like a dog maddened with rabies. He littered the floor with stuffed animals he got from his boy's room (which he tore apart), spreading them all the way down the stairs and to the kitchen.

"JJ," his cousin whispered anxiously, "what is he doing?"

They were watching from a crack in the boards on the upstairs landing.

"I couldn't tell you if my life depended on it," JJ muttered drolly.

"What? Does your life depend on it?" Moby asked, trembling in terror. Maybe dogs *are* as bad as parrots!

GG jumped up with a shriek.

"Your life! Does it? That means mine, too!" he howled.

"Get a hold of yourself, guys!" JJ snapped. "It's only an expression."

"Oh," muttered GG.

"I always think being careful is best. Because of Toby," explained Moby (unlike GG, he did not feel embarrassed by his response).

GG was (slightly) displeased at his outbreak.

Tolkien sauntered over to the landing.

"I can hear you guys, you know," he said.

The mice tentatively climbed out of their hiding space.

"So... do you have rabies?" GG asked nervously, "because if you do, you should probably leave."

JJ rolled his eyes.

"What's rabies? Do parrots get rabies, too?" Moby asked.

"Please ignore my ignorant cousin, and GG, if he had rabies, he would be mad and unable to hear reason. And as you stated, I know nothing about parrots, Moby," JJ said.

"Why would he be angry?" asked GG, his ears twitching…

"Oh, my Lord," muttered Tolkien, "really, mice, can you stop bickering so I can tell you what is happening?"

The mice stopped the incessant chatter and gave Tolkien their full attention.

"As things stand," he began, "as was per our original plan, if you remember, now that my boy has left, I am going to go over to the other house and bring back Knightley and Jake."

The mice stared at him silently.

"Alright," said Tolkien, brimming with irritation, "I know I said be silent, but what are you staring at me for now?"

"Well," said JJ, "we are waiting for an explanation of why you were running around and throwing stuffed animals everywhere."

"Ahh," said Tolkien as he settled himself comfortably on a neat pile of stuffed animals.

"That is so I can take a short power nap with the smell of my boy before my arduous journey," he answered, promptly falling asleep. He even began snoring.

The mice stared at him and then looked at each other.

"I still don't get it," whispered GG.

Jake looked at the sleeping form of Tolkien and told his cousin,

"Well, the closest thing to an explanation I can come to is that nothing is as soothing to him as the scent of his boy, and he needs that kind of comfort before going on a relatively dangerous expedition."

They sat, staring at the supine body of Tolkien.

"Now what?" asked a restless GG.

"Now we wait," answered JJ, himself starting to doze off.

"Until what?"

"Until he wakes up," murmured JJ, his eyes half closed, "and we see if he wants us to go with him."

"WHAT?!" shrieked GG and Moby in unison.

JJ shot up, startled into wakefulness by their shriek.

"What is wrong with you?" JJ whispered ferociously, "Can you ever be reasonable? Maybe you guys are the ones with Mad Dog disease."

GG began to open his mouth to holler, but JJ quickly covered it with his hand.

"GG," he began, "of course, you do not have Mad Dog disease, and please, please, stop screeching for no reason. Actually, even if you have one, don't screech, shout, holler, or even yell."

GG nodded, and JJ removed his paw.

"There really is no reason for us to go," GG said.

"He probably won't ask us to," JJ responded, resting his head back on the wall, "but we just don't want to leave him to go off without being here, right?"

"Yeah, I guess. I still don't want to go," GG whispered.

It was completely silent for about twenty seconds. In those twenty seconds, GG slid down against the wall next to

JJ. He accidentally grabbed JJ's tail instead of leaning on the floor. JJ hollered in pain, and Tolkien jumped up, barking.

"What, what?!" The startled dog shouted, jumping around, looking for the danger always around the corner.

JJ stood up, nursing his bruised tail.

"I am so sorry, JJ," said GG, "I was just trying to be quiet."

"I know, I know," said JJ, "it's okay. Sorry, Tolkien."

Tolkien, sitting calmly now, said, "It is alright. I had to go now anyway."

"So," said GG hopefully, "you don't want us to come with you?"

"No, no," Tolkien said, "I am sure you would only get in my way, all due respect."

He stretched his body, and the mice scattered out of his way.

"You are so much more frightening when you do that, Tolkien!" GG squealed.

"So sorry, Mice, no harm intended."

"Hopefully, we will never have to see you intending us harm," JJ said, almost jokingly. But he could only joke so much about such a terrifying image.

"Yeah, because that would mean you have rabies," Moby remarked in deadly earnest.

"Well," Tolkien said, as he began to go down the stairs, "I promise you, if I do get rabies, you will be gone so fast, you'll hardly feel it."

The mice stared at him open-mouthed at his callous rendition of their possible demise. They watched as he ran out of the house to begin his journey.

"Is he joking?" asked a terrified GG.

"I don't think so," answered JJ turning around. He smiled at his cousin's unwarranted fear, "I don't think so."

"I can't see how anything could get worse!" Moby exclaimed.

If only he knew that Tolkien would return home with an extremely unwelcome guest. And then the mice would see how much worse things could get.

Chapter 26: Sunny's Plea

Tolkien ran down the driveway at breakneck speed in the direction of the other house.

I just want to make sure everything is secure in our neighbors' homes as I go on this very insecure mission, he thought as he ran up every driveway he passed. *I need to know I am returning to everything the same way I did when I left it.*

He followed the directions he gave to Knightley, and in two hours' time, he saw the vibrant blue roof. He stopped at every possible place to drink water to ensure he had enough energy. He also had to ignore the yapping of other dogs (One little dog dared to say that Tolkien's boy was incompetent, which was why Tolkien was running away! That deserved the bite Tolkien soundly gave him).

He trotted quickly down the driveway of the blue-roofed house until he was a few feet away from the familiar front door. The woman of the house was fidgeting nervously in front of the doorway.

He stopped to smell the air. A cat, maybe another cat farther away? Definitely a mouse. A scared mouse. And finally, the bat. His ears perked up, and he could hear low voluble talking. He made out the frequencies of Knightley and Jake. The mouse's echolocation pitches were high, indicating fear.

A moment later, Sunny came trotting out, passing in front of the woman.

"Oh, Sunny! Thank God she got it!"

Tolkien saw the cat carrying a mouse. He started to growl.

"I can't believe I was too late! Put him down, you infernal feline!"

Sunny began to whine, taken totally by surprise by the dog.

"Oh, stop it, you waste of space, Canine," she finished by, with relative gentleness, placing the mouse down. Jake, still trembling with anxiety, looked between the two creatures warily. *That is Tolkien! This is weird,* he thought.

Tolkien looked between the mouse and the cat. *This is Knightley's doing,* he thought. Sunny was usually confident, but there was something different about her demeanor this time. She was almost afraid. Not quite terrified. She and Knightley must have reached an understanding.

"Well, well," said Tolkien, "why so nice to a mouse and not up a tree like you usually are when I come?"

Sunny began to whine uncomfortably.

"Why you are taking so much pleasure in vetting me is suspect," she hissed. "Explain yourself, please."

Tolkien sat and stretched his body out as though he were relaxed.

"Just relax, Feline. I am not really a threat," he said.

Sunny jumped backward, hissing.

"Your tail and ears are showing you're ready to pounce. Why wouldn't I be wary, Canine?"

Tolkien stood up, his tail and ears relaxing.

"Well, you are acting out of character. You were being gentle with the mouse. Why shouldn't I be... perplexed, Feline?" Tolkien asked.

The tension left Sunny's body.

"Uhh, I don't understand what's happening here," squeaked Jake, standing between the cat and dog.

"That is because the configuration of creatures communing together sends conflicting messages to all present parties. Even the ones you cannot see observing."

Tolkien, Sunny, and Jake all jumped at the sound of Knightley's voice.

"Come on, Knightley," said Jake, "there is no need to sneak up on people, even though I am still very relieved you came!"

"Well, your reaction is not surprising after the ordeal you have been through," said Knightley, becoming instructor-like.

"Thank you, Knightley," responded Jake, glimmers of his audacious banter, "and I am glad that this experience has done nothing to stop your infatuation with schooling."

Knightley preened, spreading his wings. Jake rolled his eyes. Tolkien and Sunny stared.

"This is kind of freaky," Sunny muttered. "So unnatural."

"Tell me about it," Tolkien responded, "you should see them at home. Do you know the mouse brings him his food?"

Sunny began snickering.

"Yes, Knightley told me how Jake saved him, which is not odd in our world for animals to help each other, but they are still weird."

"Well, as a dog, I appreciate loyalty, but that is because I am a dog, and that is my natural instinct. On the other hand, a mouse taking care of anything is almost unheard of, let alone a bat," Tolkien shook with silent laughter.

Now the mouse and the bat stared in shock.

"We're weird?" Jake held Sunny's gaze unflinchingly. "How do you explain this freaky image of a cat and a dog conversing and laughing together?"

"Yes," Knightley fixed Tolkien with a questioning look. "It borders on disturbing!"

Sunny began grooming, nonchalantly, as if she had no care in the world and wasn't wondering how she was being friendly with a dog and actually happy about it!

"You know," she said, "we are standing here, this 'odd configuration of creatures,' in plain sight, and someone is going to notice. The children here are very perceptive, and they are always at that window."

Simultaneously, they turned their gazes to the wide expanse of the window on the top floor.

"What do you think we should do now, Knightley?" Tolkien asked, at the same time as he was thinking-appalled-that he felt so convivial with Sunny, whom he only ever previously liked because she was fun to torture.

"Well," Knightley gathered his wings. "In light of the present circumstances, I believe we should all go home."

"All?" Sunny, grooming a spot that she thought she may have missed. She looked all around her, immediately shifting her gaze, desperately trying to cover her longing to go with this oddly constructed group of misfits.

"Oh no!" Jake began trembling. Really this is overkill!" He immediately paled at his choice of words.

"Oh, come now, Mouse, you have been here for twenty-four hours, and I haven't done a thing to you." Sunny began preening. "Well, except teasing you a bit."

"There are other mice, good mice who live in the original Clement Valley Mice property." Standing like a security guard, Tolkien barked, adding emphasis to his defense. "Would you be able to contain yourself?"

Sunny's eyes took on a (rather intimidating) green glow.

"Yes, but there are also one-hundred-and-twenty-five acres of forest and the different animals that only a forest has. I promise I will be occupied."

"No, no, no, no, no, no, no!" Jake uncurled his body and began hollering. "This is insane!"

The bat began to hover over Sunny.

"Why should we trust you?" Knightley's voice was deadly serious.

Sunny eyed him, her fur standing a little on edge (she could not help reacting to his intimidation techniques).

"You are a creature who values the use of logic and sound thinking, and you can see, by way of reasoning, that I have proven myself calculating and not wild. I have done nothing, though the opportunities were many."

Knightley floated away from Sunny, hanging from the branch on the low-lying bush in front of the house. He was a few feet away, and his favored position indicated his approval.

"That is quite true," he said, "what do you think, Tolkien? Or should I bother asking, considering your newfound camaraderie?" He asked Tolkien, the closest thing to a smirk his elevated status allowed for on his face. Even Jake began to snicker.

"Well," began Tolkien, bristling, wanting to deny the irrefutable fact, but finding himself unable, "I think she has proved herself able to be reasonable and not completely mal-intended."

Jake began bouncing around.

"No one seems to want my opinion," he said.

Jake glared at everyone around him.

"I will just tell you anyway."

"In all honesty, you didn't give anyone a chance to ask you. But that is a good indication that you are feeling much better. And how did you phrase it? Ah yes, 'I can see you are returning to your old rambunctious self'."

Knightley finished his statement with a self-satisfied chirp.

"So, now that I am listening will you ask me?" Jake asked.

"Yes."

"Oh, come now, Knightley," Sunny purred, "that is not much of a comforting reply, and I am a cat!"

Jake looked at her.

"Jake, my poor rodent, does that answer your question?" Tolkien responded. He gave the sulking mouse a fond lick.

"No." He said. He turned around, giving the animals his back.

Knightley calmly floated off his perch to level himself directly before Jake.

"My dearest friend, for that you are," he said, "and I am not good at teasing and showing love at the same time, although I must say that I do not quite understand how people seem to think those two expressions of emotion can correlate. They are actually quite contradictory-"

At this point in his speech, Jake interrupted Knightley.

"As far as I am concerned, you managed to convey both of those emotions pretty well, if I am going, to be honest," Jake said.

Looking at this odd configuration of soon-to-be-travel-companions, Jake thought he was mostly happy. More importantly, he felt safe.

"I think it is okay. Anyway, Clement Valley has tons of rabbits to keep her occupied!" he declared.

"Good then," said Tolkien, "now I just have to find a place to sleep, and we can leave tonight."

"Yes, sleeping is a good idea," said Knightley. Floating back to the low-lying shrub, he continued, "We need to rest so we can travel."

"Well, I will just haunt my normal rounds and take my cat naps," Sunny said, contentedly grooming herself, "and reassure my family so they'll never suspect anything."

Jake was eyeing her nervously, still not 100% trusting of her.

Sunny opened one eye.

"Jake," she purred, "are you still nervous with me?"

The mouse began to fidget but maintained eye contact.

"You tell me," Jake answered. "You only said you would be occupied in the Valley."

The cat began to laugh.

"You do pay attention! And are pretty brave for such a little thing."

The bat began to sing.

Curling herself up to block the sound, Sunny said, "Okay, Bat! I get it!"

Tolkien began to growl in irritation.

"Can the three of you stop?" he asked, his head still resting on his forelegs, "And we haven't even started the trip."

In a few moments, the three travelers were sound asleep.

None of them saw the white owl soundlessly watching from the tree, a mere ten feet away.

Chapter 27: The Owl and the Crow

The crow smelled the dying foal. He followed the stench until it led to a wooded patch. The baby deer lay at the base of the tree trunk, fighting to breathe. The keen eyes of the crow zoned in on his dying prey.

Suddenly, his stiff feathers began to tingle. He could feel an owl.

Soundlessly, the barn owl perched on a branch just above the crow.

"You are not welcome here," the owl rumbled.

The crow cawed, his morbidly black feathers not even ruffling.

"And you are a fool for threatening me. Where there is one crow, there is a flock. You remember what happened to that last unfortunate owl who threatened a crow, don't you?" The crow said. His voice penetrating and grating.

"But of course," responded the owl. The owl did not fidget, but it was as if his huge eyes grew as he stared into the depths of the crow's black eyes. "But how do you think your flock would fare against a flock of owls?"

The ebony bird began to rearrange his feathers. He forced a laugh.

"I think there are not enough of you to make a flock. On the other hand, I only have to call out a signal, and your entire flock of owl friends," at this point, he paused to let out a derisive squawk, "will be swarmed."

The huge glowing, orange eyes on the crow, the warm-colored owl descended, coming level with the crow.

"I will say again, you are not welcome in this valley. We have laws we abide by."

"No," said the crow, defiant and angry, starting to fly away, "you do not own the sky or anything beneath it, and we will not abide by rules created by other than our own. And our rules are everything is fair game."

The owl spread his wings, lifting himself directly above the flying crow again, and said, "Do not seek to step onto a territory you not only have no right to but do not understand. You will not fare well."

The owl flapped his wings, and without a sound, he went to gather his forces.

Chapter 28: GG, JJ, Moby, and Kitty

"It has almost been twenty-four hours," JJ said, standing on the window ledge. "Something has happened or is going on."

GG scampered over and jumped up next to JJ.

"What does that mean?" GG said. His voice was only one octave away from a screech.

Moby flitted quietly between them, his tiny body fitting neatly.

"Calm down," said JJ. Trying his best to not show his real level of anxiety, he consoled GG with:

"It could mean anything."

GG began jumping up and down, accidentally knocking JJ off the ledge. JJ's arms flew into the air as he began to fall, hitting Moby on the way down.

"Ow!!" JJ shouted.

"That hurt!" Moby exclaimed.

"I am so sorry, JJ," GG shrieked.

JJ stood, dusting himself.

"It's okay, GG," he said, offering Moby a hand.

"Thanks!" Moby said.

GG sat down, his tiny legs dangling off the ledge.

"No, it's not okay. Nothing is now."

All of a sudden, something rammed into the window right behind him. The force of the hit knocked him down. He fell right next to JJ and Moby. The three mice stood beside each other, staring straight into Kitty's brown eyes.

"What is wrong with the two of you?" She shouted. "We've all grown old here and understand too much for us to act like we've never seen anything! And stop giving a bad example to the little guy."

The mice hugged each other.

"Now stop acting like a bunch of scaredy cats. Sorry for that comparison, but honestly!"

"Kitty, we do know we have been through a lot together," JJ started to say.

"We?!" Kitty hollered, "*we* have not done a thing together. I have nearly been killed, have had several babies, and I am a grandmother and a great-grandmother. So, we don't compare. The only thing we have in common is our place of birth."

"Yes, of course, that's true," JJ acquiesced. GG just trembled so much that he was nearly shedding his fur. Moby stood still as a statue.

"And stop shaking GG," Kitty said, taking a bite of the wall, "even though you are right that nothing is right." She paused her chewing at the wall.

At that statement, GG simply fainted, whether from acknowledging the truth of his words from a terrifying Kitty or just Kitty's terrifying presence.

Kitty continued chewing the wall but stopped and said, "Hey, little guy, stop being so scared!"

Moby stared at her in horror and toppled over.

JJ stared at the lying forms of GG and Moby. He thought he might use his companions' unplanned nap to hear the rest of Kitty's foreboding statement.

"Now that they are temporarily indisposed, what do you mean everything is not right?" JJ asked.

"Well, that is heartless," Kitty chastised, "why don't you wake up your cousin and the little guy, so they can hear?"

JJ shifted nervously because, truth be told, Kitty scared him, too.

"I was asking you to think about them. I am scared whatever it is you want to tell us will make them more... uncomfortable."

Kitty took another bite out the wall.

"Kitty, with all due respect," said JJ. He climbed up the window ledge again. "Aren't you afraid this wall will fall if you keep eating it?"

"That would be the owners' problem," she said. "And if it gets that bad, they'll fix it. They need this encouragement. Can't you see how much us goats encouraged this place's slow but steady renovation?"

JJ did not say what he was thinking out loud, that he didn't think it was fair, because he could hear the stress the owners went through when they had to renovate. He personally appreciated it when the house became loose around the boards and felt the owners should just relax. But he certainly wouldn't be the one to tell this veteran that. Or anything, for that matter.

"So," JJ said, "what was it that you wanted to tell us?"

After another bite out of the wall (Jake could not tell whether that was to prove her renovation point or just hunger), Kitty said, "There is more than one thing. First, there is a wounded baby deer, which brings up the second issue. There was an angry crow here trying to eat it. And now there is a vengeful crow planning on getting back at the owl who stopped him from eating his prey."

"A crow? And then the crow is going fight the owl? That is war! And owls are terrifying by themselves, and crows are heartless *and* terrifying and mean, and a war is just, it's just, well, there are no words to describe how horrible!" Came a shriek from a now wakened GG.

JJ put his face in his hands.

"That worked better than the cold water I was going to dump on your face," JJ mumbled.

"I heard that, JJ," GG said. Turning to Kitty, he asked, "What are we going to do?"

"Owls are probably scarier than parrots," Moby said. His voice was barely a whisper.

"We have to help that poor little deer," Kitty said. *The little guy is terrified! And I can't deny that owls are scarier than parrots. Whatever parrots are.* Kitty thought.

The mice stared at her. Waiting. She slammed her horns against the wall. Once again, the hit threw the mice off the ledge.

"What on earth was that for?" stuttered GG trying to regain his balance.

"I don't know. Why don't you pass out again?" Kitty snapped.

"Hey, that was mean," JJ said.

"Very," GG said. He lowered his head, embarrassed at his glistening eyes.

"Yeah, even Toby was not that mean!" Moby chimed in.

"Who is Toby?" Kitty asked.

"The parrot," Moby told her.

Kitty began banging her horns on the wall.

"I am sick of parrots! Little guy, you have to get over your obsession with them! What are they anyway?" She said.

Moby tried very hard to hold his ground. Literally.

"They are just a bird," he said, "a talking bird."

Kitty was confused.

"What do you mean, 'a talking bird'? We all talk!" She did not like dealing with things she did not know firsthand. And better than everyone else.

"Oh, no." JJ buried his head in his hands. "Here we go."

Moby fidgeted. "Well, he speaks like humans do." In an attempt to appear respectful in front of the terrifying goat, he folded his hands in front of him, head down.

JJ and GG covered their ears in anticipation of a resounding crash.

Sure enough, Kitty began to wildly pound the window. It not only assaulted their ears but shook the wall.

"Like humans!" She shrieked. "What an unnatural, un-animal thing to do! Do humans like them better than they like the rest of us??"

I hope Moby does not say what I think he is about to, GG thought.

Sure enough, Moby said what GG thought he would.

"Well," Moby squeaked more than mice naturally squeaked. "Definitely, the girls from this house were very charmed."

JJ and GG did not think they could make their bones flatter than they already were, short of disappearing.

"How dare they!" Kitty wailed. "It is not our fault that we cannot talk like they do! It is not our fault that we speak to them in our language! They should feel honored!"

Moby straightened.

"Miss Kitty," he began, "we are animals, and you are not being very nice to us! And you were mean to GG!"

Yes, he was trembling like a leaf, but he understood enough in his short stay here that the animals of Clement Keep were good and just to one another. He did not genuinely fear Kitty. Maybe a little, as she was an unbridled animal with her emotions.

GG and JJ were very impressed with Moby.

"Hey," JJ whispered. "Nice to have you here with us."

"I am so glad you are on our side and are a mouse!" GG said. JJ rolled his eyes.

Kitty calmed down with several bites on the wall.

"I am sorry, GG," said Kitty, almost remorsefully, but the mice didn't believe she was really that sorry. GG scowled at her, emboldened now with his fellow mouse's bravery.

"If it is a war we are looking at," she said, and her worry this time was real, "I am afraid that we are not in a position to hold Clement Keep."

If the mice were worried before, now they were terrified. Kitty had been in battle and survived attempted threats to her life. And she said she was afraid. So, what should that make them? JJ came out of his petrified stance and leaned against the window.

"So, what does that mean we should do now?" he asked.

"First, come outside here, so I don't have to keep shouting," Kitty snapped.

GG started to sway.

JJ, without looking at his cousin, put his paw on his back to keep him straight and told him firmly,

"GG, don't you dare faint again!"

"Okay, okay, but I am really scared to step outside!" GG grabbed JJ's hand. Then he abruptly took his hand out of JJ's and caught hold of Moby's. Moby beamed.

"Oh, please don't do that, especially in front of her," JJ muttered.

Kitty's horn hit the window again.

"Would the three of you just come out already??"

JJ put his arm across GG and Moby's shoulders.

"Come on, we'll go out together," he told his comrades.

They slipped underneath the door frame, facing the horse pasture. On the balcony, which had somehow become Kitty's headquarters, they saw how much bigger than them Kitty was. And it was so cold!

"Welcome to the outdoors," said Kitty as she sat down, "and be prepared to hear the owl hoot in a few seconds."

"Oh my God." JJ did not even bother catching GG this time. It was all he could do to not swoon himself.

"Is he going to do this every time something scares him?" Kitty asked, stomping her hooves and trying to control herself from stepping on GG.

"Probably," said JJ. He leaned against the door, afraid that he might faint, too.

"I'm up, I'm up," said GG, staggering around. "How much longer?"

"Hopefully soon, so that the two of you will freeze, and he and his fellow owl from the other house can come and talk to you, and we can make our plan," Kitty exclaimed.

The mice froze in their places. They were stunned.

"What?" asked JJ.

"We should have never come out. It was a trick," whispered GG.

"I am curious about owls," said Moby.

"Oh, my Lord, I know that mice are scared creatures, but no one ever said anything about being scaredy cats!" Kitty yelled.

"Cats!" JJ hollered back, shock snapping him out of stupefaction. "Now that is a hit below the belt. No mouse wants to be compared to a cat! I know you are older and have seen so much more, but cut us some slack, will you?"

As if the owl could hear that bold statement, he hooted, and the mice froze.

Chapter 29: The Owls, the Mouse, the Cat, and the Dog

The sky turned dusky, and Tolkien's eyes opened. He was on his feet in half a second, only controlling his instinct to bark because he saw something almost imperceptible.

"You saw it, too," Sunny whispered. Tolkien nearly jumped out of his skin and, this time, could not control his startled growl.

"What is wrong with you? You scared me half to death! Go up a tree somewhere!" He growled.

"Well, I would," Sunny responded, "but I am relatively sure that the owl is there."

"An owl?" Tolkien asked. He wasn't that worried. Except he was worried for Jake and Knightley, to whom owls were a danger.

"Two, actually," Sunny said. Licking herself, she appeared almost casual while she imparted nerve-racking news.

"Two?" Tolkien said. His growl was no longer muffled. "That is not normal, and how do you know?"

"You are right. It is not normal, any more than me and you talking is normal," Sunny said. She was still licking her fur.

Tolkien was watching her groom herself and feeling nervous and out of place.

"Would you stop doing that? No one is that clean," he snapped, taking a swipe at her.

Sunny meowed in objection.

"You would say that because you are definitely not clean at all!" She retorted.

Tolkien was offended.

"I will have you know I bathe almost every day."

"Yeah," Sunny snapped back, "in a filthy, still water pond."

"It is not still water! There are springs of the cleanest water people pay for," Tolkien proudly informed her.

"Which is why someone should tell them you take a bath in there. Almost every day, which contaminates it, no one would buy it. I mean, dogs are notorious for their stench!"

"Alright, alright," Tolkien said, "we have bigger things to deal with now. Owls hardly ever leave their territories, much less communicate unless to establish their ownership. And you did not tell me how you knew."

"Cats and owls have rules with one another. We share the same prey, so we simply recognize one another's turf. This place is understood to be for us cats."

"Yes..." Tolkien prodded, "what does that mean?"

"It means," said Sunny, her eyes slits of green, "something is wrong."

Tolkien put his head down between his paws, groaning.

"We don't have time for anything wrong right now!" He said.

"They are not hostile, and one of them is from The Valley."

"What?" Tolkien barked.

Now it was Sunny's turn to take a swipe.

"Would you be quiet!?"

"Well, how about sheath your claws?"

"You shouted before I struck, and don't be a baby. My claws barely scraped you," Sunny told him.

"If and when the mouse and bat wake up because they will shortly, they are going to feel the owls, and they will lose it, and *then* you will hear noise," Tolkien informed Sunny.

"Actually, Jake will freeze, so he won't be a problem. But his guard dog-bat might be."

Tolkien buried his head in his forelegs.

"And then what?" he muttered.

"I resent being called a watchdog, Sunny," said Knightley, who had silently floated over. " With all due respect, Tolkien."

Tolkien gave an affirming low-throated grow.

"No offense taken, bat guy."

"Ahh. You are not so forgiving, Tolkien," Knightley said, "I can tell you took offense by your ears. Standing straight as soldiers, they are."

Tolkien grumbled.

"You're right because being a guard dog is one of the highest forms of honor, and you should feel nothing but grateful," he said.

"Well, aren't the two of you sweet," said Sunny, "and while being a guard dog does place you at a fancy rank in the human world, a cat is honored in our animal world. We are admired for carefully evaluating the situation and only doing what is least destructive and most gainful for ourselves."

Knightley and Tolkien stared at her, open-mouthed.

"What?" she asked, once again grooming herself uninterestedly.

"Really, you make me reconsider our decision to include you in our trip," said Knightley.

Tolkien started to laugh.

"No, Knightley, she's just feeling left out," he said, playfully shoving her, after which she let out a startled yowl.

"Tolkien! I'm not one of the 'guys' that likes being shoved, affectionate or not," she purred. *I am one of the guys!* She thought, secretly happy.

"There is an owl here," piped up Jake, wandering into the discussion. All of the travelers turned to look at him.

"Why are you so calm?" Tolkien was astonished at Jake's calm reaction.

"Dude, I just had a training crash course with Sunshine over here," Jake said, "and nothing is more terrifying to a mouse than a cat."

"I am so glad to hear you say that," came a resonating, velvety voice.

So silent was the advent of the snow-colored owl, not a single member of the group heard. She and her grey feathered companion were smart, flying downwind, so none of the animals smelled them.

"Yes, I must agree," agreed another voice, gruff and sonorous, "though I must challenge your assumption that nothing is more terrifying to a mouse than a cat."

Jake's fur almost paled in color with horror. *It is true!* He thought, *Owls are even more terrifying! What was I thinking?!*

The grey owl began laughing.

"Despite the appearance and general habits, I am not here for any meal. I am here to gather an owl fleet to challenge the crows violating our Clement Valley's rules."

"Of what do you speak, my silent friend?" Asked Knightley.

"He means," said the snowy owl, "the crows have come onto your land and tried to eat a baby deer when all outlying lands know that carrion is not to be touched in Clement Valley. The crows foolishly threw down the gauntlet."

"Do not start to howl," Sunny told Tolkien, who had stood, bristling in righteous anger.

"How did you know?" Disappointed at not being able to unleash his feelings, Tolkien sat down, sulking.

"Cats know things," said Sunny, "and I was right."

Tolkien scowled.

"So," Jake said, relieved but still horrified, "we are all on the same side?"

"The fact that you and your mice relations living in the Clement house are all still alive speaks for itself. Do you think that I don't know you each by your scents?"

"That is not comforting!" Squeaked Jake.

"I don't think he is trying to be comforting," said Tolkien.

"No, I am not. I am trying to ease your little mouse heart by letting you know Clement Valley animals protect their own." Replied the grey owl.

"Owls are very different than parrots," said a wide-eyed Moby. He spoke in a hushed whisper, standing stock still, barely able to breathe, looking at the owls.

"The real question is, Grey," responded Tolkien looking at Moby inquisitively while addressing the owls, "why are you here with another owl who is not from the Valley?"

With that stealthy silence, the snowy owl flew to perch next to Grey.

"Your Clement family is connected to the Clement family here. I am thereby connected to the valley," she said.

"The crow declared war on the owls," Grey said.

"The age-old war between owls and crows is legendary. It has been kept at bay for more than two decades, and it is not surprising for it to surface now," Knightley said.

"Please tell me you have some sort of a plan, Bat Guy," said Sunny, "It is getting very dark."

"We have come together, Ms. Snowy and me, to devise a plan," Grey said.

"Good. I am assuming all of my worst nightmares have a plan that includes protecting me from themselves," snapped Jake.

"You would think someone in as...vulnerable...a situation as yourself would learn respect," Snowy said. Her eyes were flashing dangerously.

"Now, no need to terrify the little one. He has been through a lot," said Grey, "and we are on the same side. No need for fighting in the ranks. We have the same enemy."

"What is your plan now?" Knightley asked.

"We should all move now, to the valley," Grey said, "me and Ms. Snowy already went before you and introduced ourselves to the Clement Valley mice and Kitty and informed them."

"What? Where? Kitty?" shouted the group of travelers.

Jake mustered enough courage to step forward.

"I am sure they were terrified!" he said.

"And if they were not informed, they would still be standing in front of your home with Kitty. They would have been meals for vengeful crows! They were surprisingly composed, by the way, and Kitty boldly took them on," Grey comforted them.

"She is rather formidable," inserted Snowy, "and I acknowledge that as one of the more intimidating breeds of mammals."

"Good," said Tolkien, feeling very crabby that these two flyers were stepping onto what he considered his domain, "we are glad you saved everyone."

"They are waiting for your return," said Grey.

"Who's is in charge now?" asked Sunny, her sense of importance and excitement dimming in the presence of the two-winged interlopers.

"Our plan is not much changed," said Knightley, calmly establishing his authority, "we only know we have additional soldiers. We should continue on to the valley as planned."

Snowy looked at Knightley intensely.

"Under whose authority do you claim leadership over this mission, Chiroptera?" she asked. She spoke quietly, her voice threatening.

"That would be a Clement Keep Animals consensus," responded Knightley, spreading his wings.

The atmosphere thickened. Tolkien and Sunny began whimpering, and Jake burrowed himself in the dirt.

"Now, now," said Grey, "let us not forget we are none of us enemies. We are in this fight together."

The travelers relaxed their tense muscles.

"Yes, indeed we are not," said Knightley, unfurling his wings, "let us continue on our way."

And now, a very strange legion of animals, sharing only to defend the sanctity of their land, set out.

Chapter 30: GG, JJ, Kitty, and the Owls

What happened before the owls met the dog, the cat, the mouse, and the bat

The mice stood, petrified.

"Oh, come on now, you know they are safe. Buck up!" Shouted Kitty.

I know this is a far cry from mice capacities, she thought.

"And I'm right here. No one will do anything to you when I am around."

"That is bold of you, Goat," said the Snow colored owl perilously.

The mice were beyond terrified.

"Kitty," whimpered GG.

Kitty looked down at the trembling mice. She banged her horns on the post. No one scares her, Clement Animals!

"Now you listen here, Owl, don't you come here in my home and dare think to threaten me and my friends!"

The Owl looked at her in surprise. *She is a feisty one. Clearly, she has been through enough to make her fearless.*

The Grey owl, who lived mostly on the oak tree in front of the house, cleared his throat uncomfortably.

"Snowy, this is Kitty, who I may honestly say I have watched grow beautifully and survive the unimaginable."

The snow-white owl looked intensely at the old black and white-haired goat.

I think I like her, Snowy thought.

"Maybe you can tell us now what is happening?" JJ, seeing no real threats—despite owls' aptitude of generally being deadly—asked the crowd.

"Don't draw so much attention to yourself!" GG said in a very loud whisper.

"They may not be able to control themselves for that much longer," Moby added, standing still as a statue.

"Alright, that's enough, mice, at ease. Now," Kitty said, turning to the owls, "what is the plan?"

"We came only a little before the traveling party, and you should expect them shortly," said Grey.

"So, Tolkien, Knightley, and Jake should be here soon!" Shouted GG, ecstatic.

"Yes, and don't forget Sunny," said Snowy. Though her voice was low, the intended group of mice heard.

The mice became very still.

"Sunny? Who's Sunny?" asked Moby.

"What do you mean, 'and don't forget Sunny'?" JJ asked.

"I mean," answered Snowy, "Tolkien and Sunny have become fast friends."

"That is crazy!" shrieked GG, "How could he!? He went there to teach her a lesson and save Jake from her!"

"Maybe she is like a talking parrot," Moby pondered.

"Suffice it to say, they found common ground," Snowy said.

"Alright, that is enough," said Kitty, banging her horns against the wall, "if Tolkien has become her friend, or more likely just decided not to kill her, he wouldn't bring her back without some confirmation that she wouldn't do anything."

"So, Tolkien is bringing a cat home," said JJ thoughtfully, "and I do trust him, but there must be another reason."

"Yeah, he's just selfish," said GG, crossing his arms defiantly.

"No, that cannot be the reason, and don't forget he went out originally to save your kin," said Kitty as she seated herself comfortably. "Don't be such ingrates," she added.

"I think Tolkien is trustworthy," said Moby. "He would defend me from Toby."

JJ and GG looked at each other.

"I think you are traumatized," said JJ, putting his arm around Moby's shoulders. GG came over and hugged them both.

Kitty rolled her eyes.

"Do you remember saying we could not handle a full-blown war against the crows?" asked Grey.

JJ's eyes widened.

"You heard that?" he asked. Moby loosened himself from the loving hugs.

He looked at Grey, his eyes wide.

"You are like a parrot!" he said.

"Probably not that smart," said GG.

Grey chuckled.

"Do not underestimate an owl's hearing capacity," he said. "And do not worry, little newcomer, I am honored with that comparison, though I cannot talk in human words."

"Though we do not talk, we are endowed with communication abilities that are never misunderstood," Snowy added. GG flinched at the glow in her huge eyes.

Moby felt the grey owl would protect him from his previous scary companion, so he did not worry. That much.

JJ just wondered when this exceedingly uncomfortable gathering would be finished.

"No need to be so foreboding about it," he muttered, "you are terrifying. We get it."

"So now we are gathering our forces," said Kitty.

"What is the first thing we are going to do?" Snowy asked Kitty, deftly granting the goat the order of command.

"First, we have to take care of the baby deer."

"Where is it?" asked JJ.

"Right beneath the tree on the right side of the horse pasture," Grey said.

"Which one?" GG asked.

"The one where they used to be before winter," said JJ. Sometimes his cousin could be so daft.

"Well, that's silly. Why would they go all the way back there?" asked GG.

JJ rolled his eyes.

"Don't be a dunce, GG, the horse pasture where they are now."

"The point is," Kitty cut in, "that the deer has to be taken care of, and we have to decide who will take care of it."

"It must be either yourself or Tolkien," said Snowy.

"Or the horses," Kitty said. "The first thing the baby will need is water; the horses are near her and have water close to them. And hay to keep her warm."

"Very good thinking," said Grey.

"Who will talk to them?" asked JJ, a little nervously, "They are kind of prized creatures. What if they feel it is beneath them?"

"Nonsense," said Kitty, standing up proudly, "I am a prized creature! I will talk to them."

Chapter 31: Kitty and the Horses

"Do you think she'll ask?" Dune asked Maggie, plotting ways to get to the hay.

"Yes. Since when does she not ask for whatever she wants?" Maggie snorted, standing patiently.

While trusting her companion's ability to think out of the box when it came to getting food, she was highly vexed at his obsession with filling his belly at almost any cost.

"Are you irritated? You sound irritated," said Dune.

"I am too old and tired to be irritated."

"Maybe because you are too old and tired, you are actually irritated," Dune told his longtime friend.

"Maybe you are irritated because you haven't had a moment's worth of patience in your entire life," Maggie said, nipping him.

"Maggie, I hate it when you do that. And Treat Lady told you that's not nice. And for the record, I display a lot of patience when she brings us water or hay, and that is saying something!"

Maggie knickered in agreement.

"She does take forever, doesn't she?"

Maggie turned, walked towards the right side of the pasture, and stuck her head over the fence. Dune plodded along after her.

"How is she doing?" he asked.

"His breaths are coming shorter and shorter," Maggie answered. "We have to find a way to get water to her and some hay."

"Exactly my thoughts," Kitty said, standing behind them and startling them both.

"Oh, for heaven's sake, Kitty! You'd think you'd get over the thrill of startling us already!" Maggie snapped.

"But it's so fun," Kitty said, snorting with laughter.

"Yeah?" Dune, leaning over the fence to nip at Kitty, said, "You should just be grateful that we took you in after everyone else was sold!"

"Yes, I will never deny that. Since we are already on the same page regarding the baby, let's get down to business," said Kitty.

The horses turned their attention to Kitty.

"Well, we definitely hate most of the crows and don't like to see them breaking Clement rules," said Dune, shaking his head and tossing his hair defiantly.

"No need for a show, Dune," snapped Maggie. "No one doubts you!"

"As I said, old and crabby," said Dune, a safe distance from Maggie's snapping teeth.

"Do all the animals on this farm have to bicker?" Kitty complained crabbily.

"Hey! It's a sign of our love! That's how we do things in Clement Valley," Dune exclaimed proudly.

"I don't think that is a healthy form of communication," Kitty said, "and I have raised generations—"

"Oh, come on!" the horses said together.

"You used that same story for every single aspect of life, from animals, all the way to humans-" began Dune.

"Humans are animals," interrupted Maggie.

"Fine, from owned animals to the animals that are owners," Dune doggedly refused to accept correction.

"STOP!" shouted Kitty.

The horses obediently tempered down.

"Now that we are all calm," continued Kitty, "we have to figure out how to get this water to the deer."

"You can push it with your head like you did before, and the girls loved it," came a squeaky voice from between the tufts of grass.

All pandemonium broke loose. The horses reared and neighed. Kitty began gauging the dirt with her horns, and the mice, well, the mice just began running around in circles.

"What are you doing here!" hollered Kitty, "You cannot, ever, especially with horses, startle them! Especially mice!"

"It is a good thing I didn't start to hoot," Grey's eerily quiet voice came. It was too much for the horses. They had barely just gotten their bearings. So, they began galloping around the pasture in terror.

"Did you really think that was the right time, Grey?" asked Snowy. She stared at him, dumbfounded.

"No, I knew it wasn't. It was just too irresistible," he said, "I mean, it was set up so nicely." He could not stop laughing.

Snowy glowered at him.

The mice were frozen.

Kitty just seated herself on a grassy patch.

The Clement Keep animals had no idea what they were getting into.

Chapter 32: The Clement Valley Animals and Bambi

"What were you saying now, GG?"

GG stood as straight as he could, with all his trembling.

"Dune pushed the water trough to the edge of the fence before with his head, and he could push it to the fence by the deer now, and Kitty could help her drink," he said. All the tentativeness in the world could not save him, he knew. So he was as bold as he could be.

JJ stared at him, pleasantly surprised by his cousin's forthrightness.

"I wish I saw that," said Moby.

JJ nudged GG approvingly, "Nice work, cuz," he whispered. GG beamed.

Dune eyed the little creature, a cross between terror and irritation.

"They did compliment you a lot, Duney boy," Maggie told him. "Go ahead, push it over now. There's a boy."

Dune obediently placed his head in the trough and began to push it over to the fence.

Kitty walked over to the doe. She gently placed her cheek next to the doe.

"Come now, little girl," she whispered, "you need to drink some water."

"Too weak," the doe mumbled.

"Nonsense, the whole farm is helping you now," Kitty told her. "The water is right here and will give you some strength."

"I can't," the doe repeated.

"Sure, you can," Kitty told her, "grasp my horns, and I will help."

The doe obediently grasped the horns with her weakened hooves. Kitty began pulling the doe to the water as gently as she could.

The mice watched the whole endeavor expectantly.

"She really is a good mother," said GG.

"I can see that," Moby said, admiring Kitty.

"She always was a good mom," murmured JJ.

"And a good grandma," GG added.

The horses stood by the gate, anxious. Their ears standing straight up, they snapped at the admiring mice.

"Really, you should have some respect for us," Dune bit out.

"Oh, come on, Dune," Maggie said, "you know we aren't afraid of mice."

"Really?" said GG. "I always felt kind of powerful thinking that we could scare big things like you guys."

Dune glared at him.

"Don't get too cocky, squirt. I could still squash you," he remarked.

"That's enough, and don't get too cocky yourself. I could still bite you," Maggie told Dune.

All the while, Kitty was tipping the water trough while the baby deer sipped weakly.

"Feel better now?" she asked.

"Yes," the deer responded, "a little."

Kitty grabbed a mouthful of hay and put it in front of the baby.

"Here you go now, eat a bit of this, whatever your name is," she said gently.

"Bambi," said the deer, "call me Bambi."

Kitty laughed.

"Quite fitting," she said.

"Bambi?" asked JJ, "How does she know about Bambi?"

"Every animal knows about Bambi. He's a legend," said Dune.

"He's a boy," said GG matter-of-factly, "and she's a girl."

"But she is an orphan who watched her mother die, which is the material point," said Maggie, bending down to graze.

Bambi startled.

"My mom's not dead! Don't say that!" she cried out.

"Here they come," said Grey.

Everyone jumped at the sound of his voice.

"Every time, you old owl!" shouted Kitty, startling the already startled horses.

"None of you guys should ever come out!" Yelled Dune.

"Really, everyone should stop acting so surprised when we all know we are the only ones here," said Snowy.

"Well, almost," she finished, raising her sights to the returning travelers trotting and gliding up the driveway.

The mice started to bounce in excitement until they noticed Sunny, and then they practically flew behind the safety of Kitty, clinging to her legs.

"That is probably not safe," Bambi said.

The mice, naturally, jumped in fright. Bambi started to laugh softly, wobbling on her legs.

"Guys, I really can barely move, and the deer have never had an issue with the mice. Especially baby deer," she said.

"How would you know?" asked GG.

"The same way you know that you are afraid of cats even if you've never seen one," said Bambi.

At that moment, Tolkien came barreling up to the mice and began licking them in greeting.

"How are you guys?" he asked.

"And what about me?" Kitty asked. "Why don't you ask me, you big oaf!"

"Who could forget about Invincible Kitty?" Tolkien asked, promptly giving her an affectionate lick.

"Quite disgusting," Knightley said, shuddering. "Why you think everyone appreciates that form of affection, Tolkien, is beyond me."

"I would give you the same honors, my Equus family friends, but you are far too tall, but know that I am happy to see you," Tolkien told the horses.

"I think you should greet me as you always do," said Dune, looking at Tolkien with thinly veiled irritation. "A series of sharp, aggravating barks that you know drive me to the point of almost stomping the life out of you."

"There is no need for that type of violent speech, Dune," Knightley said, smiling reassuringly at Bambi.

"Please, Dune, we are in a time of war, *and* we do have company," Tolkien told Dune sagely. Dune began pawing the ground.

"Come on, Dune," Maggie told him, "for once the canine is right."

"Where is Jake?" JJ asked, ignoring the big animals' squabbles and wanting to greet the returning hero.

"Right here," Jake said, climbing from behind Tolkien's collar. He jumped down and threw his arms around JJ, GG, and Moby.

"You did it!" they cheered.

"Oh, the stories I can tell!" he said. He was laughing and joyful at being back, having undergone an adventure that would have been difficult for most animals.

"You mean," said Sunny, sidling up between the mice, "we can tell."

The petrified mice stared in awe at Jake and the cat.

"Jake," they began asking, "why aren't you terrified?"

Jake did not feel quite comfortable, but there was no way he would show his trembling body, being the returning hero and all.

"She's not so bad. I mean, she didn't eat me! And what's a little teasing between friends?"

He finished his bold statement by running to the safety of Tolkien. Sunny glowered at him. She did not like to be toyed with.

"Well, aren't you a little trickster," she muttered. "Don't worry. I won't tell them how terrified you were."

"If I thought you were cool because you could play ball, you have really shown me up with your crazy boldness!" Said GG.

"Oh, come on, I'm just happy to be back and that it is over!" Jake said.

"Hey, where'd Moby disappear too?" Jake asked. JJ and GG started looking around.

"He's right here," said Tolkien. They all looked at Tolkien. He was standing in front of a pile of hay. A tiny hand popped out, waving. Tolkien stared down. This little mouse always confused him.

"What are you doing, Whale Boy?" he whispered.

Moby crept out of the pile.

"I have never before been around a cat, and it is absolutely terrifying," he said, dusting himself off.

Sunny straightened. "You have an interesting scent there," she said. She began to creep over.

Knightley floated over to her and began humming. Sunny yowled, swiping at him.

The cousins and Jake started laughing. Quickly, they scampered over to Moby.

Tolkien left the mice to rejoice in their reunion and turned his attention to the newest member of The Valley group.

"I can see Kitty has taken care of you, as her wonderful maternal instincts would have her do," he told the bashful yearling.

Kitty stepped in front of the little deer.

"Listen here, young lady, you have only just recovered and still have a ways to go before you can be up and about."

The old goat turned to face Tolkien.

"And you, you mangy mutt, just move on."

Tolkien growled but obediently walked away.

"'Kitty," Bambi said as she gingerly sat down, "what about if the crows come back?"

"Oh, they definitely will," Kitty told her, "but do you see all these animals? We have all come together because of you."

Bambi looked around. The four little mice, the dog, the cat, the bat, the two owls, and the two horses all looked back at her, smiling.

And then she began to whimper, looking at the sky. All the animals followed her gaze. Their startled reflexes turned on while they looked to the sky.

"What is that?" came the collective cry.

Chapter 33: The Surprise

"It's a crow!" Knightley exclaimed.

The flying crow did not seem quite as balanced as he rode the sky as any flying creature normally would.

"There is something wrong with that bird," Grey stated.

The blackbird neared, and the observers could clearly see what was wrong. It was missing a leg and one badly torn wing. They watched, silently, suspiciously, while he landed in front of them.

"Much as I wish it were not the case," the crow said, his deep, almost unreadable black eyes looking at them, "I fully understand your unfriendly judgment of me."

No one denied his supposition.

"Be that as it may," he continued, "I am not your enemy, nor do I condone your enemy's actions. As you can see, I have no leg. I was born with this deformity and separated myself from my murder very early on. My deformity placed me at a disadvantage, not because it made me incapable, but because they disparaged and despised me because I looked different. After I left them, I concentrated on my flying capabilities and very shortly became the best flyer in the sky. I did not show off in front of any of them. Indeed, I made sure I was far from them for several years. But they were watching, unbeknownst to me.”

He shifted his position and saw that their eyes had softened. Their interest was piqued, but they are still reserving judgment if need be.

“Two nights ago, after I determined to fly to let you know that if you needed my support in defense of Bambi,” he said with a nod to the yearling, “I would be here for you. They attacked me by surprise, but I fought them off ferociously. My advantage was that they did not know how strong I was.”

Now their eyes were filled with admiration.

“Wow,” said GG, awestruck, “and I thought you were cool, Jake.”

Jake gave him a look and then shrugged.

“Me too,” he whispered, his eyes smiling.

“So,” said Knightley, “you come bearing bad tidings and help.”

“And news,” said the crow quietly.

“What might that be?” asked Tolkien.

Kitty still stared suspiciously, her mothering instincts causing her to hover over Bambi protectively.

“Her mother is still alive.”

"What?" asked Dune.

"How do you know that?" Maggie questioned.

"That is good, but where?" asked Tolkien. Seeing himself as the soldier of the troop, he wanted practical information.

"We'll find her!" GG volunteered.

"No, we absolutely will not," said JJ, putting a calming arm around GG. "We would be dinner for the other crows in less than a second."

"I know where she is, naturally," said the crow.

Jake left the sanctuary of his kin and walked over to the crow.

"Why?" he asked, his brown eyes looking into the unfathomable black eyes.

"Because I know how senseless and brutal a murder of crows can be. Look what they would do to even their own?" he answered.

Jake nodded.

"And they killed my mother," he said, lowering his gaze to the ground, "because she would not kill me when I was born with this deformity. At least I can save another baby from losing its mother."

After this sincere explanation, the Clement Valley Animals were deferentially silent.

Maggie plodded over to the gate and lowered her head down.

"Crow," she said, "as you are now a part of the Clement Valley Animals, please feel free to use my hair to build a nest."

The crow laughed.

"Thank you, Maggie. Please feel free to call me Sun Flower, everyone."

The silence he was met with now was muffled as one, and all stifled their laughter.

He glared at everyone.

"Sun Flower?" squeaked GG, "What? Is that your way of making a statement?"

By this point, the entire group was guffawing.

"No," said the crow, "my mother told me that every year I would come back stronger."

All laughter ceased immediately.

He turned respectfully to the old horse and said, "I am honored, Maggie, to use your hair."

"Well, now that we are all finished with introductions," Dune said, still a little uncomfortable with the faux pas, "what is the plan?"

"The most relevant question is, do we know when the crows are planning their attack?

And then, with equal relevance," Knightley asked with a nod towards Bambi, "how does saving her mother fit in with that?"

"It's a good thing the family is traveling," JJ said, "it gives us room to act accordingly with all our plans."

"The mother should be attended to first," Sun Flower said, "considering we cannot be prepared per se for the attack. We must be ready at all times."

The animals were nervous.

"Where is she?" asked Tolkien, his response erring once again on the side of practicality, "that is something we don't have to wait to find out."

"There is a little stream, roughly halfway up the hill," the crow responded. "She is lying right next to it."

Tolkien walked up to Bambi.

"Bambi, I need a scent to follow," he told her, "and I am sure you carry her scent, so if I may?"

He leaned down and sniffed her until he was sure he had the mother's scent and tore off up the hill.

"Well, that was strange," said Bambi.

"Very," the cousins agreed unanimously.

"Not really," said Moby, "Parrots talk, and dogs rely on their very powerful sense of smell."

"What do we do?" asked GG.

"We are mice. We rely on our sense of fear," Moby answered.

"Well don't we have an answer for everything," JJ rolled his eyes.

Chapter 34: Tolkien and the Mother Deer

All Tolkien felt as he sniffed through the tangled trees was that he was in his element.

If they think they can come on my turf and disrupt our way of life, he thought, *they've got another thought coming! Do they think there is not a wise creature among us?*

Tolkien's ears perked up when he came closer to the source of the scent. Gingerly, he weaved his way towards the sound of the stream making its way down the hill. He finally saw the deer lying at the edge of the stream, shielded from sight in the twisted trees.

"I've come to take you to your daughter," he told her. She shifted at the mention of her daughter.

"She's alive?" she whispered.

"Yes," Tolkien answered, "and doing well."

The mother deer heaved herself up, only to collapse again. Tolkien trotted to her quickly.

"Ma'am, you cannot move just yet," he said, "we have to stop the bleeding first."

"We?" she asked. She laughed weakly at Tolkien's serious demeanor.

"Metaphorically speaking, of course," he responded with an answering grin.

He began sniffing around for yarrow leaves to help the blood coagulate faster. He found a patch of the yellow leaf and pulled them up. Gently, he began to tear them apart with his claws. After he ground enough of them, he took a whole leaf and placed it on the deer's wound.

"Ow," gasped the deer, "what are you doing?"

"I am not the dog of an EMS person for nothing," he said, placing firm pressure on the wound,

"or living in a house with a family who really talks a lot about everything."

"So?" Said the mother deer, trying to escape the pain the dog inflicted.

"I learned things," Tolkien answered. He watched her, listening for her breathing to indicate the pain was lessening. He waited for several minutes until he felt the seeping of the blood abate.

When he was assured that her breathing was becoming more regular and the bleeding was stopping, he removed the leaf and began to sprinkle the powder of the leaf onto the wound.

"How are you feeling?" he asked.

"Like there is a bullet inside me," she responded. Her voice was significantly stronger.

"I don't think we should move it just yet, and I also don't think I should take it out," Tolkien said.

"How will it get out?"

"I am sure when my pack gets back, they will deal with it."

"No!" She shouted. Overestimating her strength, she immediately flopped back in pain.

"You cannot react like that physically!" Tolkien exclaimed, "You will start bleeding again."

"They will slaughter me," she said.

"No," Tolkien said firmly, "they will not. They will see your baby and leave you be."

"How are you so sure?" she asked.

"Because I know them and their positions about mother deer and their babies."

"What," she snapped, her voice bitter, "did you hear them say, 'never kill a deer that is a mom'?"

"There was one time when they went out hunting. When they returned, they realized it was a doe. It was clear she was nursing. The family was very upset," he said. The mother deer eyed him.

"Is that all the assurance you can offer me?"

"That should be all you need to hear. They would never knowingly kill you or kill a baby deer."

Tolkien stood confidently, defending his pack's honor.

"What the owl said was right," he reminded her, "we have our own rules here in the Clement Valley."

Chapter 35: Sun Flower

"Alright, Daisy," Jake said, idly tossing his acorn up, "You have to tell me how hard it was to deal with your whole crew with a name like that."

The animals were sitting around waiting, albeit nervously, for Tolkien's return from the mother deer. A question that only Jake would have the audacity to ask (Knightley was fuming with his protege) was exactly what was needed.

The crow's black eyes held Jake's gaze unblinkingly.

"That's kind of freaky," GG whispered.

"What? The crow's death look, or Jake's unnecessarily provocative question?" JJ said.

GG thought about the question.

"Both," he said.

"Yes, I did get laughed at." The crow responded, "But not for that long."

"It's a good thing you didn't talk in human words and used only mouse words," Moby said, feeling very awkward.

And yet Jake remained unintimidated.

"Yeah, I can totally see you making sure no one messes with you."

The crow continued to study the bold little mouse. He was confident in a strange way.

"Please forgive my impudent friend," Knightley said. He glided over, almost humbly.

I now see why Jake seems so sure of himself, the crow thought. *The bat is sort of his house trainer.*

"It was not so difficult to establish my authority with the rage I had that they killed my mother."

Jake lowered his head respectfully.

"I am very sorry you had to see that. Or even that it happened in the first place," Jake said.

"How did you conduct yourself after that horrendous episode?" Knightley asked. GG, JJ, and Moby inched closer to Sun Flower.

"That must have been horrible," GG said.

"I never knew my mother either," he continued, trying too hard to create common ground.

"Well," said Sun Flower, his obsidian eyes hard as slate, "I knew my mother very well."

"What he is trying to say," JJ said, putting his arm across GG's shoulder to let his cousin know he wasn't alone in facing this potential predator, "is we are very sorry for your loss, and we welcome you to our family." Moby opted not to talk and simply nodded his head.

"Thank you, Mr. Sun Flower," Bambi spoke up, "for coming to tell us that my mother is alive."

"You know," said Dune, "lots of us animals lose our mothers at a young age."

"And not so many of us adopt them by demand," Maggie said, nipping him.

"Hey, I keep you young," Dune told her, "and went with you to see your child."

"Actually, it was the owners' grandsons," she responded as she bit him for good measure.

"I am a mother, a grandmother, and a great-grandmother, and I keep all of you in line here on this farm! Even the humans!" Kitty hollered, ramming her horns into the horse pasture fence.

The owls remained silent during this whole altercation, sentinels watching over the property.

"And here he comes," said Snowy.

"In a rush, too," added Grey.

Tolkien came to a skidding stop in front of Bambi. He bent down to give her a quick lick.

"Disgusting," said Sunny.

Tolkien growled at her.

"Hey, don't be a hater," he told the cat and then turned his attention to Bambi.

"That was from your mother."

"Oh, that was wonderful!" The baby deer exclaimed.

"I must go back now to her so she is not alone. I have to find a way to move her closer to us here until my boy gets back and he can take care of her," Tolkien said before he shot back to protect the fawn.

"Well, isn't he the gentleman," said Sunny, trying to be snarky but unable to hide her admiration.

"I, for one, am proud of him," Kitty said. "Such a testament to my upbringing."

The animals just stared at her, wondering how Kitty always managed to turn every good thing back to herself.

"Do you ever feel abandoned by his owner, considering you were his first baby?" asked GG. JJ buried his face in his hands.

"I can't keep saving you from yourself, cuz."

"She was?" Moby asked, his eyes wide.

"Abandoned?!" Kitty shouted. "Do you remember how he would not sell me? Came outside to stop the buyers from taking me?"

"Yes," said GG in a small voice.

"Oh, that is so sweet!" Moby said.

"Good," Kitty said, sitting down. Things were peaceful, everyone adjusting to the new circumstances and solidifying their places.

Chapter 36: The Murder

"We never should have trusted him."

"You mean we should have finished him off? Oh, wait. I forgot. You couldn't do it when you had the chance."

"He's a traitor! Us crows are nothing if we do not protect our family name!"

"You and the family name! You are the one who couldn't keep us together—killing his mother in front of him! It's a mother! Of course, that would turn Mr. Legless against us!"

"Yeah, and then he became Super Crow," added the third crow flying in.

"Alright, that's enough. What are we going to do with the Clement Valley Animals?"

The most senior crow began to cackle.

"We will do what we do best. Gather our forces and swarm them tomorrow at dawn when they are most tired."

"I don't know," said another crow, "haven't you been watching the Valley Animals?"

"What? You mean that there are lots of different kinds?"

"Mostly snacks; Just bite-sized mice," another crow chimed in. The crows began laughing.

"Literally breakfast on a platter." The crows on the nearby oak tree branch began flapping their wings in appreciation.

"Make the call," said the unruliest of them all. "It is time."

"You just can't wait to get back at him, can you?"

The senior crow cawed.

"We will not swarm them at dawn. That is what they will be expecting. We must do it at a time when they would least assume we would be out. The middle of the night."

"And leave our roosts unprotected?" one crow shouted.

"We will be finished shortly," said the senior crow. "They will not expect us."

"No one beats me without retribution," said the angry crow. "No one."

Chapter 37: The Goat Pasture

Tolkien sat, his ears pointing straight up. He could hear the cackle of the crows.

"Nasty creatures," he muttered. "So tribal!"

"They are a force to be reckoned with," the doe said.

Tolkien abruptly stood up.

"Good, you are awake! Let me see your wound." He plodded over to her. The entrance wound was still red but not pussing.

"How do you feel?" he asked. She stood up and moved a few steps.

"Good, all things considered," she answered.

"Then I think it is time for us to go down to Spring Hill Pasture."

In the said pasture, the Clement Valley animals were dozing in the warm late morning sun. Or trying to. It had been a long night and a busier morning. Besides the owls in their natural sleeping spots, the mice were exceedingly uncomfortable.

"Why didn't we go back inside?" asked Jake.

"That is a very good question," GG concurred.

"Maybe if you could stay still and stop fidgeting wherever you slept, you would be able to get a good day's sleep for once in your life!" JJ snapped.

GG was hurt.

"That was uncalled for, JJ," he said.

JJ popped his head out of his neat hay burrow.

"Look," he said, "I'm sorry, GG, but really, if you burrow yourself in the hay and stop moving, you'll feel warm. Honestly, I always heard that hay was warm, and it's true. Give it a try!"

GG climbed into a patch of hay. He squirmed a bit and then nestled.

"It is nice," he agreed, "we should bring some back with us for our nest." His muffled voice barely reached JJ, but it didn't matter. JJ was already sleeping.

"Finally," Jake muttered, "they just never stop, those two."

"You might be totally amenable to me eating them now," Sunny murmured.

Despite himself, Jake grinned at his former torturer's words.

"Yes, because we know I've never lost any sleep because of you," he said.

"No, I just gave you nightmares," Sunny retorted.

"It is pertinent that we rest. Living inside has turned us from crepuscular creatures into primarily nocturnal ones. So that being said, "we need to secure all the sleep we can by returning to our instincts. Who knows what tomorrow holds for us," Knightley said while circling the troops.

"Come on, Grim Reaper," Jake groaned, "how can anyone sleep with you creeping up on us and giving us lectures on things we can hardly understand? What is crepuscular anyway?"

"I think you should decipher the meaning of crepuscular from the context. I am sure you can. You are very capable." Knightley's well-intended comment only further infuriated his ward.

Jake's eyes were blazing.

"I am sure it means something like: 'get used to not sleeping enough'!"

Knightley, on the other hand, was delighted.

"See now! I know you always underestimate your vocabulary comprehension. You are not exactly precise in your definition, but it is very much tied with wakefulness in the dark, dimly lit hours of dusk and dawn. That being said, having become accustomed to living in the house dulled our once finely-honed reaction to light or lack thereof-”

“Just stop!” Jake screeched, fury causing him to fully enter into wakefulness.

“It does not matter now,” said Knightley coldly. He was highly offended that his words of knowledge were not being accepted gratefully. “Here comes Tolkien and the mother deer.”

Bambi jumped up.

“Mother!” She cried out, bounding over to the gingerly walking deer. She pulled short abruptly.

“Your hurt!” She said. Her mother laughed softly and came close to her baby, nuzzling her.

“No, no, Tolkien took very good care of me and brought me down to Spring Pasture,” she said.

Tolkien looked away.

“No, it was the least I could do,” he said, “at least until the owners get home.”

Kitty, stately and proud, walked over to the deer.

“Spring Pasture?! What on earth is ‘Spring Pasture?’ This is The Goat Pasture! Oh, if only Deja and Vu were here!”

As a whole, the animals took a step back.

Except, of course, GG.

"Yeah, the owners couldn't handle them. They were so happy to get rid of them!" He laughed at the memory, oblivious to Kitty's blazing eyes.

"Nope," said JJ, shaking his head. "Not cleaning up after his mess."

"Listen, you little mammal. You aren't fit to lick their hooves! They are legends among us goats! They taught us we don't have to stay in all the places people trap us!"

"Are they like parrots?" Moby asked. He was holding his hands together, not really understanding what was happening.

GG had enough sense of fright not to respond to Moby.

"This is the Goat Pasture! Built by Osama," Kitty defended the pasture's original namer.

"Though we did kind of crush him when we got out. But that was his fault because he played that video about the escaping goats." She started laughing. The animals were beyond frightened. The maniacal look in her eyes terrified them.

"They were something else," she continued, "and then when Osama said don't show it to them, we had to watch from the window!"

"Kitty," began Tolkien, "we understand your feelings, but can you take it easy?"

The animals waited silently. Kitty *harrumphed* and sat down. The storm had passed.

The mother deer smiled.

"Clearly, I can see you were the perfect mammal to have taken care of my fawn," said the mother deer, "and I thank you."

Bambi stood up and nuzzled her mother.

"I am worried about you, Mother," she said.

"Do not worry, my dear. When the owners come home, Tolkien assured me his boy would take care of my wounds." Her mother put her face alongside Bambi's.

"If I may," said Sun Flower. He flew carefully over by the mother and daughter.

The doe was visibly startled.

"It's okay," her daughter comforted her. "He is safe."

Tolkien walked over by the deer.

"If you may what?" He demanded.

"Yes, what indeed?" Knightley added. He was not quite certain yet of this interloper.

The crow began to spread his wings slightly.

"Do not try intimidating me," the crow said. "Especially as I have shown nothing but friendliness."

"Forgive us, please," Knightley said. He lowered himself slightly beneath Sun Flower. Tolkien followed his lead, sitting down.

The crow relaxed his posture.

"As I was saying," he continued, "my beak is very suited to pulling out things lodged in places. I can pull out the bullet with little pain."

"That is a great idea!" Kitty said.

"Very thoughtful indeed," Snowy said.

"And a good way to establish your loyalty," Grey said. "Good foresight!"

"So, the rumors are true," remarked Maggie. "Crows are exceptionally smart."

Dune put his head through the bars of the pasture gate. Sun Flower bristled.

"Hey, don't startle, Flower boy," Dune said. He began to knicker.

"Do not call me that. Ever." The crow snapped his sharp beak.

"Relax. I was just going to tell you to feel free to use my hair," Dune said.

The crow's feathers relaxed.

"Thank you, Maggie," Sun Flower said. "And yes, Dune, I will make sure to use both your hair when I begin to build my nest."

"So," GG's eager voice, "are you really going to take the bullet out?"

Jake looked at JJ.

"Can your cousin ever just remain silent?" Jake asked him.

"Based on whatever little I know of him," Moby said, a part of the family now, "I don't think he can remain silent."

JJ reached behind his head to grab the hay.

"No. And to think I really believed I could sleep now," JJ groaned.

The crow turned to look at them. GG had a decision to make. Either he would stay where he was, which was not where the crow was looking. Or he would be noble and go stand by his relatives. His ears began to twitch.

GG made his decision. He tore over to his kin.

"I am being loyal!"

His voice came out much squeakier than anticipated. Jake clapped him on the back.

"Your loyalty is much appreciated," he told his frenetic new friend. JJ rolled his eyes.

"I was going to say," the crow said, "yes, I am going to take out the bullet in answer to your question, GG."

GG jumped up excitedly. "He said my name!"

"Are you really going to take it out?" Asked the Doe.

"Time is of essence in this kind of situation. An infection could develop, and my beak is thin enough to swiftly pull out the bullet with minimal damage. My feathers have antibacterial properties that could fight a developing infection. I will pluck them from myself and line the site of the bullet wound."

"Or we could pluck them for you!" GG said, offering his (genuine) services. Sun Flower turned a stone-cold gaze on GG.

"No, you may not," he stated.

"You certainly sound quite capable," remarked Knightley. He hovered near Sun Flower. Whether in admiration or from insecurity was unclear.

"And educated!" Tolkien said, by way of apology.

The crow nodded, acknowledging the praise and accepting the apology.

"So, what should I do?" asked the mother deer, short of breath. Her heart rate was increasing with her anxiety.

"Just sit down comfortably," Kitty told her. "I am sure Flower Boy here will be very helpful."

Sun Flower snapped his beak angrily at Kitty.

"I hate that name," he said, almost snarling. It is very hard to snarl with a beak, but his eyes had wonderful capabilities. They were so powerful a creature could almost feel like they were bit by the sharpness of their gaze.

Kitty turned away from his sharp eyes.

"Miss Deer," he told the mother deer, his eyes conveying gentleness and confidence, "if you just stay sitting, I will come and remove the bullet swiftly."

She took a trembling breath and nodded.

"Okay," the mother deer complied.

The crow hopped over to her. Her eyes widened.

"How do you do that?" she whispered.

He smiled, or rather, his eyes smiled.

"Because I have no legs?" he asked. "Well, if you notice, the bottom of my wings are where my feet would be. So, I simply push slightly using them."

"Wow," said the fawn in awe. Actually, all the animals were impressed.

Sun Flower bent his head over the bullet site. He delicately inserted it into the skin with the very tip of his slightly opened beak. The deer flinched ever so softly. In a few seconds, he raised his head, his beak holding the bullet.

The animals cheered in each of their own very different ways (Tolkien barked; Kitty bleated; The mice squeaked; The horses snickered).

Sun Flower rose abruptly.

"Are you out of your minds? We cannot draw attention to ourselves! We are already too conspicuous," he reprimanded the animals.

"What does that word mean?" whispered GG.

"It means very obvious," Snowy responded from her perch. GG jumped.

"Maybe you could try being conp-consic-conus. Whatever. Just… you could try not to be so sneaky!" GG finished his very trying statement and plopped down, exhausted from fear and from trying to say a word he simply could not.

"Just as you cannot help but be terrified almost all the time, I cannot help being terrifyingly silent."

GG grumbled, accepting defeat (in a terrified sort of way).

"I, being as I am the unchallenged leader of the Clement Valley Animals," Knightley said, his wings beginning to spread in a statement of superiority, "understood the importance of being inconspicuous and therefore was utterly silent."

Jake began to snicker. "Come on, old man. I think you have finally met your match in Flower Boy here. Crows have been around for a long while too and have the advantage of that special view 'flying affords', right?"

Snowy bristled.

"As do I!" her eyes were flashing.

"There, there, comrade," Grey said, "sometimes the greatest heroes are the unsaid ones. Our silence can make people forget our existence. Until it's too late." His eyes were burning.

"I think everyone should just be happy that we all managed to save my mom!" The fawn said. She burrowed her head in her mother's neck shyly. The doe placed her cheek on her baby's face.

"That's my girl," she said.

"Now that we are done stating how important we each are (*I am a horse! And taller than all of them!*) She thought to herself.) we should try to figure out when these crows are

most likely to attack and begin gathering our forces,"
Maggie said.

Chapter 38: The Forces

"There are more than two of us, you know."

Dune stood still and regal. His slender, graceful form made one think of delicacy and beauty in its highest form. Unless you got to know him, then you would understand that, yes, he is sensitive and perceptive and beautiful, but like most sensitive creatures, there is a flip side. "Not the time for your bucketload of insecurities, Dune," said Maggie.

Dune began to paw the ground.

"I'm just saying, it's not just owls and crows who have huge families. We have the two of us, the Polanski horses, the Killoy horses, the Martin horses, and I am sure several others."

Maggie raised her head from grazing and looked at Dune.

"Dune, do you understand anything about crows? Or anything, for that matter?" she asked.

Dune was, not surprisingly, hurt.

Maggie huffed.

"I am sorry, Dune," she said. "I am anxious."

Dune put his head on her neck.

"It's okay. I am nervous, too. But I do understand something about crows."

"Do you now?" Maggie said. She was a little skeptical.

"They do not like a lot of noise, especially if it comes from an unsafe source."

"And?" Maggie prodded.

"No, really! There is a murder of crows who live about half a mile in the outskirts of the Western Pasture," said Dune.

"How do you know that?" Maggie asked. She felt angry that she did not!

"Come on, Mag, sometimes I am more inclined to know this stuff because I am a male who needs to be prepared to take care of things!" He began bucking. Maggie reared up.

"Do not talk to me about being male and defending things. My son is a stallion!"

"Hey, no need to stick it to me. I am still a stallion." Dune said, settling down.

"Well..." Maggie let her voice trail, "Cryptorchid Stallion, you mean."

Dune reared up and began galloping around the Goat Pasture. He skidded to a halt directly in front of Maggie.

"Even if I was completely gelded, which I say again, I was not. I would still be a domineering male!"

Maggie seated her body down on a sunny patch of grass.

"Calm down, Dune. I practically raised you. So sensitive! I know your dignity is intact. It is just too tempting to tease you."

"Are you sure you don't remember the chatter about Rumor?" Dune asked.

Maggie lifted her body off the ground. The Sun was moving anyway, taking away its warmth. She walked a few paces, facing the Western Pasture. She looked beyond the field and into the dark depths of the forest.

"I only remember him barking and the coyotes howling."

"The coyotes were calling the crows to come to partake in their meal," Dune said.

Maggie neighed softly.

"Yes, it makes sense that scavengers would work together."

"This means the coyotes will come with the crows," Dune said.

"Which means, Dune Boy, we have to call the horses."

Dune neighed and bucked.

"What on earth?" Kitty shouted from outside the fence.

The dozing animals got up in varying states of frazzle.

"We have an armed guard to prepare," Dune cried out.

Maggie plodded over to Kitty.

"Kitty, we are calling for the horses."

"Guys," GG whispered, "will there be a stampede?"

The three mice glanced at each other. They were apprehensive. They were clearly worried. They were possibly terrified.

GG began to sway.

"So, it is scary," he moaned.

Moby opened his mouth. JJ immediately covered it.

"Do not talk about parrots," he muttered. Moby slumped.

"Parrots are just a huge part of how I think," Moby said in an undertone.

"Well, we don't have parrots here or anything like them," said JJ.

"I don't know if I would say that," Jake said. He put his arm around Moby's shoulders. "I personally think that Bald Eagles are like them a little. They don't talk, but they are around and intimidating."

"Yes, GG," Knightley remarked, "it is scary indeed. Even without parrots or bald eagles."

Jake perked up.

"Knightley, can you call other bats?"

"Now, what an ingenious idea, my little friend," Knightley said.

"So, can you?"

"No."

"What?" Jake was startled.

The bat looked at him.

"Listen, my little friend. Bats are not aggressive creatures. We do not fight or protect unless directly attacked. We are only together—and a great many of us indeed—after we return home from a night's foraging. At that time, we release some energy with our echolocations turned off. Unless we are together for food collecting because a situation in nature deviates from normal circumstances, we do not function communally."

"Well, that was a mouthful," said Jake.

"I think your 'protege' is feeling insecure," said Sun Flower. *His weak spot! He does not like to be reminded that Knightley has family,* the crow thought.

GG noticed his new, usually bold, companion's discomfort. He did not like it. Gathering his courage, he spoke up.

"Well, Jake doesn't have to worry about Knightley's family. He was the one who saved him!"

He crossed his arms emphatically across his chest.

JJ scampered up to his cousin, staring at GG pointedly.

"What are you doing with your arms?" he asked.

"That's what Tolkien's boy does when he makes a declaration," GG answered his cousin.

"And Toby talks human words to communicate with humans! Does that mean we should, too? We aren't human!" Moby exclaimed. All of his little body was vibrating with the intensity of his emotion.

His mice companions were taken aback by Moby's outburst.

JJ eyed Moby.

"GG. We're mice like Moby is pointing out, not humans," JJ said. "We don't do that when we make a point."

"Oh," GG said. "Yeah, it was kind of uncomfortable. His boy doesn't use his arms to walk!"

He shook his arms, loosening them.

"Now that we are done taking care of Jake's—and clearly Moby's—emotional needs, we have to start sending out for reinforcements," Sun Flower said.

"Wait!" Knightley said. He turned to face Sun Flower.

"How do you think we should set out? Or, when, rather, based on your knowledge of crows."

The crow was silent for a moment.

"Crows will generally attack at dawn. That being said, I can only imagine that they would be aware that I would know that and act accordingly. They would change their normal time of the attack."

He paused.

"We should preemptively attack," he said.

"What do you mean?" Maggie asked.

"I mean," Sun Flower said, "that instead of waiting for their attack, we cannot be certain about except that it will be, to the best of their abilities, when we are unaware. As they say, the best offence is defence."

Besides being naturally uneasy, the animals were venturing into an unknown situation. (You have to remember that not only a large number of the group were prey, making them a naturally wary crowd, but most of them had never left the confines of the Clement property directly surrounding the house. Those who weren't living on the property surrounding the house lived in Clement House proper.)

"I don't know about the wisdom of that," said JJ. His statement was met with silence. Some of the animals were surprised (Jake and Dune and Tolkien); Some of them were horrified (GG and Bambi); Most of them were offended (Sun Flower, Maggie, Kitty, Sunny, Grey, and Snowy).

"What do you mean?" Asked the crow, leveling the little mouse with a hard stare. By instinct, JJ took a step back.

"What I mean is that it seems like an ineffective battle plan for everyone just to call their troops all at once," said JJ. "After all, a battle is about strategy."

He finished his statement boldly, despite his utter horror at the possible outcome. You must understand he really was a tasty appetizer for more than half of his audience!

"Well, color me surprised!" Said Kitty. "From the mouth of snack-sized prey." She started to laugh. No one else did. They were still marveling at the mouse's boldness.

"JJ!" Said Knightley. "I had no idea you were so well versed in the battle strategy!"

The hawk eyed him for a second. He began nodding his head.

"Quite impressive, I must agree. I am only embarrassed as I did not think of that myself," he said.

"Being mice," Jake said, "we are therefore sort of programmed to be nervous-"

"Absolutely horrified, almost all the time!" GG inserted.

"Or that," JJ said. He clapped his cousin on the back, smiling. "We know how to be safe because we are constantly aware of our surroundings and our enemies, present company excluded, and timing. Basically, we are calculatingly careful."

Moby gazed at his newfound parrot replacement.

"I am sure you could talk Human if you really tried!" He said.

Jake rolled his eyes.

"Thank you, Whaley, but I would rather leave talking Human to humans. And parrots." JJ finished his statement laughing.

"My dear friend, your insight does you well," Sunny said, walking up to him slowly.

JJ began to back away from her.

"Sunny, I can never tell when you are being predator-ish, or just having fun being creepy."

"Don't be such a spoilsport," she said. She sat down, her fun ruined. She began grooming herself.

"I was just having a bit of fun."

"You have some way of having fun, Sunshine," Jake said.

"So now that our mice friends have given us such sage advice, what is our plan?" Grey asked.

Everyone looked at JJ.

"How do we proceed?" asked the mother deer.

"Hey, Sun Flower, where do they live if we were going to attack them first?" asked Tolkien.

"I do believe he asked his mouse friend!" GG stomped his foot. "Ow," he squeaked. "It looks so much easier when your boy does that too, Tolkien!"

Moby shook his head, unable to understand GG's infatuation with Tolkien's boy. *Who am I to judge?* Moby thought. *Look at me with Toby!*

"Their roost is on Heart Attack Hill," the crow said, wondering how he got himself entangled in this bickering group.

"Yes, they would choose a place with a name like that to build their roosts," said Knightley. "A morbid group, they are."

"If we want to take them by surprise, we should have our winged comrades advance first in the middle of the night," JJ said.

"No," said Sun Flower, "I think we should start at moon rise."

"Because you believe they might be planning a midnight raid?" Snowy asked.

"In that case, we will disrupt their vestibule and put their plans in tumult," said Sun Flower.

"Very good planning, indeed," said Tolkien.

"We should make a distraction, too," Jake piped up.

"How do you mean?" asked Maggie.

"If we were able to gather the Clement Valley Mice to be there on the ground while the owls flew in, it might make it more difficult for the crows to concentrate on fighting," Jake said.

His idea was met with silence.

"That could be very dangerous, Jake," Sun Flower said, breaking the rather stunned silence.

"Too dangerous," said Knightley.

The three mice looked at each other.

"We live in their home," said JJ. His voice was somber. "Though we might not be a very long-lived creature, we have been here for longer than any other animal. Sometimes something is worth sacrificing for."

The hush was audible.

Dune cleared his throat.

"That is very brave of you," he said.

"That is insane!" Kitty screeched.

"That is brilliant," said Snowy.

"So, when the owls fly into their roost at moonrise, will the mice come simultaneously?" Grey asked.

"They should come in with the owls. A tactical maneuver." Jake said.

"How about if I just go inside the house and defend the house," GG started creeping back to the house.

JJ put his arm around GG's trembling shoulders.

"I think that's a great idea," JJ reassured his cousin.

"GG!" Moby exclaimed, "This is not the time for being cowardly!"

"OK, great," said GG. "I'll just head over there now."

"Hold on, my little friend," said Knightley. GG's shoulders slumped.

"The owls will overwhelm them in the sky and serve as the main attack and unbalancing penetration," said Sun Flower, "and the mice will be a distracting maneuver."

"We still need a secondary attack," said Sunny, "and I do not see why my feline comrades cannot join the mice on the ground."

"This is horrible," GG's voice drooped along with his shoulders.

"Not to worry, GG," said the Doe, "I will take you to a shelter with my daughter."

"Oh great, so it can be three for one taste," muttered GG.

"Another line of secondary attack will be to call the horses shortly after the crows have been thrown off balance with the entrance of the owls onto their territory," said Sun Flower.

"Above all else," said Knightley, "we will not pillage their nests or hurt their children."

"That is very noble of you, Knightley," said Maggie.

"That is the Clement way," he said.

"I agree wholeheartedly," said Sun Flower.

"We should start to inform our troops, right?" JJ said. His heart was racing, and he couldn't tell if it was from absolute terror or excitement.

Dune was pacing.

"Yes, my mousecapades, send the message to your mice comrades," he said. "I will walk over to the edge of the tree line and tell the Polanski horses and have them spread the word."

"Moonrise is in fifteen hours," said Sun Flower, "Do not forget that we have to do this planning operation as stealthily as possible."

"We should all go back to our respective places," said Tolkien, "as though it were a normal day."

With that, he sat in front of the porch, his usual spot to laze in the sun.

The mice scampered onto the porch and slid under the door.

The bat floated to and through the space in the doorway.

The sentinel owls stayed in their respective hidden spaces, their silence nearly a disappearing cloak.

The horses grazed casually.

Kitty walked to the shade of the balcony roof.

Sunny prowled, looking for an unsuspecting beetle.

The doe and her fawn camouflaged behind the piles of hay.

And all was quiet on The Clement Keep Front.

Chapter 39: An Unexpected Visitor

Now, while mice in the animal kingdom — particularly on a farm with herbivores — are notorious for their long hours of sleep, the less sleep-needy animals talked about them quietly between one another.

"Can you believe these guys need to sleep fourteen hours daily?" Said Kitty to the owls, who were also up and ready after three hours of sleep.

"Our military strategists need their sleep because of fear exhaustion," the owls chortled.

"If you wouldn't mind," Tolkien interrupted, "I prefer not to be offended by self-satisfied egotists so few hours after I have slept. And I assure you, dogs do not suffer from fear exhaustion."

He placed his head back down between his paws and snored shortly after that.

"When do you think they will wake?" Sunny asked.

"It has only been 4 hours," Sunflower said, "and we still have twelve hours left before moonrise, so I think we can give them another ten."

"What do we do for ten hours?" asked Kitty. *Goats are rather impatient creatures.*

"Excuse me!" said a squeaky voice from behind a stack of bramble.

"What's this?" hissed Sunny.

Out from behind the stack, a White-footed mouse stepped forward. For a mouse, it looked surprisingly unafraid.

"I heard all of you predators are not going to eat us, that you actually want us to help, and that all of you are safe now!" the girl-mouse was hopping up and down with excitement.

Sunny began to stalk forward.

"Is that so?" she asked, her voice threatening.

The mouse's huge eyes grew wider. And then she began to giggle. Bounding up to the cat, she said, "Oh, don't 'be silly! We are all family!" she paused thoughtfully. "Well, sort of, you are from the other side of the stream and forest and hill, but anyway, we are still on the same side!"

Sunny began to back away from this boisterous, very confident, and loud mouse.

"Well, well," said Grey, "I'd say you have met your match, Sunny."

"Maybe white feet lend to ridiculous, foolish confidence," said Snowy.

"Well, I like her," said Kitty, "she reminds me of, well, me."

Sunny snorted.

"You have never been that vivacious in your entire life, Kitty," she said.

"How would you know? You don't even live here," Kitty retorted.

"I do, and you weren't," Grey said.

"Well, I'll have you know," said Kitty, "I was a joyous kid!"

"This white-footed mouse seems... bubbly. You were not close. You would do what you wanted, no matter what, but, no, you were not cheery about it." Tolkien opened one eye to offer this critique.

"I was effervescently joyous!" Kitty hollered.

"Just because it is a fancy word does not make it true," said Sun Flower.

He leveled the newcomer with a stare.

"Why aren't you sleeping?" he asked.

"Oh, I was just so excited that it was safe outside now, and we were all on a mission together," she chattered, without taking a breath, "and then I saw you, and I wasn't scared because Mr. Grey said we don't do things like that here in Clement Valley, and then I thought-Oh!"

She broke off half a pace from Sun Flower (who was very taken aback by this little white-footed creature).

"Your legs!" she exclaimed. She scampered around him. Her head bent low to see his legs or lack thereof.

"What happened?" she asked, lifting her head to meet his gaze. Her huge eyes were sympathetic.

Sun Flower cleared his throat uncomfortably.

"It is okay. I was born like this," he told her.

"Well, well," murmured Sunny, "I never thought to see you thrown like this."

Kitty was feeling very insecure. She plodded over to the unlikely pair.

"Little mouse, it is a very dangerous time to be out," she stated. The white-footed mouse was undeterred. She started to laugh.

"Oh, Kitty! It is the perfect time to be out! And we are coming out anyway to be a distraction," she exclaimed.

"I am so happy to meet you finally," she continued, oblivious to the shocked stares of everyone around her. Kitty looked at her. The little mouse's eyes were glowing with admiration.

"Now, well, that is very sweet of you," Kitty said. Her insecurities were appeased. She could feel her matronly instincts kicking in.

"How on earth did you hear about me?" Kitty asked.

"Oh Kitty, you are famous with all the outside animals!" the little mouse exclaimed.

"That still does not explain why you are out of bed," said Sun Flower, trying very hard to stare her into submission.

"Oh, stop looking at me like that!" She giggled. "You know, another crow was flying around morning-hunting, and he was bad, but you are not like him."

The crow was suddenly tired. He did not like not knowing how to deal with a creature.

Maggie looked at the effervescent mouse almost tenderly. She really was something like a breath of fresh air. Dune was wary of her. No one was that trusting. Maybe it was a trick, and she'd have them all killed.

"Why don't you try going indoors and sleeping?" Maggie told the mouse. The mouse's eyes widened if that were possible.

"Oh," she whispered, "I've never been."

"You could meet your other mouse relatives," Kitty paused thoughtfully, "though I do not think you are related."

"They are good mice," Tolkien said, one eye opened, "they will accept you. It is really very good for you to sleep, and you will need energy for tonight's mission." He closed his eye and was snoring in a matter of seconds.

"That is a good idea," Sun Flower said. "What is your name, by the way?"

"Oh, I thought you'd never ask!" she exclaimed. She was so excited. She was jumping.

"I can't see how that would have stopped you from telling us," he muttered.

"It's Daisy. We are both named after perennial flowers, and our mothers named us after them because they keep coming back no matter." For the first time, she was not bubbly. The crow did not like how that made his heart soften.

"I think that once you explain yourself, the mice indoors will welcome you," he told her.

"And what if they don't?" she asked.

"Then just come back here," he said.

He looked at her and then told her, a little gruffly, "I think they will like you just fine."

She took a deep breath, briskly turned towards the house, and marched forward.

Chapter 40: And Unexpected Alarm

"Hello?" Daisy called out. She had slid under the house door from the balcony. Never before having slid under a door, she felt jittery.

Inside the cozy enclave in the rocks over the fireplace, GG started to shed his fur.

"JJ, there's an intruder!" he was trying very hard to whisper.

JJ turned over and covered his ears. GG stared at him, shocked. Who sleeps at a time like this? He stood up and took JJ's hand off his ears. He bent down, placing his mouth right above his ear

"JJ, somebody foreign has come into the house!"

JJ reared up.

"What on Earth is wrong with you!" he shouted.

GG scampered away from his furious cousin. He looked frightening, with his hair sticking straight up and his eyes blazing.

Moby, covered in soot, came out of the fireplace.

"What is happening?" he asked.

GG made placating gestures.

"Somebody came in the house!"

"The owners? It's their house. Who cares!" JJ growled.

"No, a different animal," GG said.

"GG," JJ said, "If it is not a bear, or a tomcat, or even a possum, I am going to kill you."

JJ walked out of his room and stopped short. There was a smallish mouse. A white-footed mouse. They generally never came indoors.

"Hello," JJ said.

"Hello," Daisy said. She felt embarrassed and very unsure of herself.

"Sun Flower and Kitty and Tolkien and Bambi and Grey and Snowy and Sunny and Maggie and

Dune," she courageously continued, in a single breath, "told me to come in here."

JJ stared at her. *What in the world do I do with a foreign mouse who seems to have befriended the entire valley?*

"Yes, of course," he said, remembering his manners, "please, make yourself at home."

"Really? she said, "Oh, they said you would welcome me, Sun Flower also said if you didn't, I could go back outside to him, but you did invite me!"

"Sun Flower told you that?" *Sun Flower?* he thought.

"He is oddly gracious like that," JJ acknowledged.

"Oh no, he is wonderful," she said, clasping her hands together. "Both our mothers named us after perennial flowers because they keep coming back no matter what."

"Your name is Sun Flower too?" JJ asked.

"Oh no," she said, giggling, "don't be silly. My name is Daisy."

"Daisy." He said. *I am going to kill Sun Flower. He knew what he was doing when he sent her in.*

GG, hearing that everything was safe, came out.

"Hello," he said, taken aback at seeing the small mouse. *A female?* he thought. *Interesting.*

"Hello," she said. She looked down, suddenly feeling shy. He was, after all, an indoor mouse.

"I am GG," he said.

"I'm Daisy."

"What exactly did they tell you to do when you came in?" JJ interrupted. His voice was stilted as if he was trying very hard to remain calm. Which he was not. Duh!

"Well, they said sleep. So, I can be prepared for the battle."

GG paled.

"Yes, I forgot about that," he said.

"Well, let me direct you to the upstairs quarters. I am sure there are much more comfortable sleeping quarters there," JJ said.

GG glanced at their warm, cozy, hay-filled enclave (he managed to bring some back inside, after all.)

"Actually, he said, it's mo-" JJ cut him off with a withering look.

"Yes," GG agreed, doing his best to appear casual, "you should meet the others anyway."

"Others?" Daisy asked.

"Yes, a mouse and a bat," JJ informed her as he began to jump up the rocks. She scampered behind him. GG followed. He had to see Jake and Knightley when they met her!

Outside, the animals conversed. Or bickered, depending on what you consider conversation. If you think conversation can mean having conflicting opinions loudly, then, yes, they were conversing.

"Why were you trying to get rid of her?" Bambi asked. "I liked her."

"As did I," Dune agreed, "but you have to admit she was... a little too chatty."

"You know that JJ, GG, Jake, and definitely Knightley will kill you. Or at least want to. Or just be very angry," Maggie informed them.

"Well, sometimes you have to do what you must," said Tolkien, not even bothering to open his eyes.

"Just go to sleep, all of you already!" Sunny snapped.

Sun Flower did not join the conversation and tried his best to keep his eyes open. *Just for a bit. She might come back,* he thought drowsily.

Chapter 41: Back Inside

"She's not a bear, at least," said GG.

"She might as well be," JJ said, sliding under Jake and Knightley's door.

Daisy slid in behind her hosts.

"I've never met a bat before," she whispered.

"Who is this?" Asked Jake, pointing at Daisy as he stepped out of his closet.

"Yes, indeed," Knightley said. "Will you introduce us, JJ?" Knightley was not happy.

JJ opened his mouth to introduce her, but Daisy decided to introduce herself.

"I am Daisy, and I am so so so excited to meet you!" she squealed.

Jake and Knightley stared, dumbfounded.

"The others sent her inside so-" JJ started to say.

"So that I could get some sleep before the battle. Sun Flower said you would welcome me," she added.

"Sun Flower," said Jake, murder in his eyes.

"Oh yes, he is so wonderful!" Daisy said.

"Sun Flower?" Knightley questioned. "The same Sun Flower we know?"

She let out a trill of laughter.

"Of course! How many creatures do you know named Sun Flower by their mothers because they go on no matter what? Well, there is me, but I am Daisy. That's why we bonded," she said.

"Bonded. Sun Flower. The Sun Flower I know does not 'bond,' " Jake practically spat out.

"Well, of course not, because he never had anyone who had the same experience," Daisy explained.

"Yes, of course. That makes perfect sense now that you have clarified," said Knightley.

Jake stomped into his closet, glowering at the cousins, and came out carrying bedding. He arranged it rather nicely, considering his level of rage, in the corner beneath the desk.

"As you came in here to sleep, and we have less than ten hours, I suggest you make yourself comfortable and sleep," he said.

"You guys are so nice!" Daisy shrieked. Knightley winced.

"My dear girl, my ears, as they are bat ears with very sensitive echolocation, they are very... sensitive," he informed her. Jake wondered if her pitch had rattled his usually wide array of vocabulary.

"Oh," she whispered, "can you just turn your echolocation off when I am in the room? I don't want your ears to be damaged."

For once, Knightley was shocked into silence. Jake was flabbergasted.

"I think you should go to bed, Daisy," GG told her. He was worried that this uncomfortable situation was getting out of hand.

The white-footed mouse looked at her new friends (Sort of. J-J's eyes were still burning, Jake's throwing hand was clenched in irritation, and Knightley, well, Knightley was still not recovered from her impertinent advice to shut down his echolocation.)

In her blissful ignorance of the havoc she had unleashed on the entire valley, she pattered over to her bed and, in minutes, was sound asleep. The other animals in the room just stood there, staring at her.

"I wonder to what we owe the honor of housing this particular guest," Knightley said.

"I'll tell you what we owe. We owe everyone who sent her in," Jake's voice was menacing as he turned his gaze to JJ and GG, "and who sent her up, payback."

"Hey, talk to him," JJ said. he pointed at GG.

GG straightened his shoulders.

"That is not fair! I was ready to let her sleep downstairs, but JJ told her upstairs is more comfortable."

Jake and Knightley looked at JJ.

"Don't look at me like that," JJ said, "I was awoken from a very deep sleep, and my thoughts were still not all together yet."

"We should not waste precious sleep-rejuvenating-time bickering. You mice are down to eight hours, and you need more sleep than the rest of us. For a multitude of reasons," Knightley declared.

JJ and GG obediently returned to their room.

"What was that all about?" Jake asked.

"Battle anxiety across the valley," Knightley said. "The chatterbox is a mere manifestation," nodding towards Daisy.

"God. Are they all like her?"

"No," said Knightley, "I think the world could not handle more like her. But it still stands to prove that sometimes ignorance can be exactly what is needed."

Jake glared at Knightley.

"I still have not had enough sleep to decipher your sentences. What are you saying?"

"I am saying that the mice are our first line of defense, and them not having full awareness of the extent of the danger they are in may give them a confidence that will behoove them."

Jake buried his head in his hands.

"Listen, Bat Guy, mice are very aware that everything is a danger to them, and the one thing that may be problematic has trust in you, unworthy planners!"

Jake finished off his claim. Shouting. Knightley remained infuriatingly calm.

"I think, my little friend," Knightley said, "you should complete your sleep."

Jake stomped off to his closet, wishing he had a door to slam.

Chapter 42: Messenger

The little blue bird flew his heart out. He had a plan. Maybe an overly daring one, but hey, no one lives forever.

"This war is making all of you insignificant animals bold," sneered a crow.

"Well," said the little bird, flying circles around the angry crow, "everything high must come low, and it's time you grudge-holding tyrants finally pay the price for killing that noble dog!"

"It is not 'grudge-holding'. It is revenge-seeking, you insignificant, little, flying insect," the crow snapped.

"Revenge for what? A dog guarding the sanctity of his pack and their regard for the lives of innocent creatures on their land?" The little bird said.

"Ah yes, the Clement Valley code of honor," the crow said.

"If we were crows, we would seek revenge, but we are not, and we only fight for what is right!" The little bird exclaimed.

"We never sought revenge for these past ten generations of crows. We only did when the owl threw down the gauntlet," said the crow.

"Do not think to play me for a fool," said the bird. "Do you think we do not know about your continuous violations of the laws here, all in the name of getting back at Rumor? You have exacted your revenge time and time again."

"Perhaps. But now we do it for all to see, which makes all the difference in the world," squawked the crow.

"And all those who see now are fighting back!" Said the bird.

The bird dove beneath the crow and bolted into the safety of the woods.

"Really," said a penetrating voice, "the animals in The Valley are taking full advantage of this armistice."

"Animals never do anything out of the goodness of their hearts," said the bird. "Our hearts are always good. We simply abide by rules, which are generally to our advantage."

"Well, well," said the owl, "and so they are."

"Still," added another owl, "it is amazing how many of our usual dinners are piling up."

"Now, let us not forget our real enemy in this riveting dialogue," a third owl said.

"I can speak for a lot of your usual dinners who would say that owls are a little low on the rung for birds of prey.

Sometimes they become the prey!" The colorful bird pronounced.

"As long as you remember, even that prey can turn you into a fine meal!" snapped the first owl.

"Alright," said the third owl, "I think we're done taunting now."

"Tell me," the second owl asked, "have you heard the latest plan during your flight?"

"In fact, that is why I came to this part of the forest. To start spreading the word of our attack at moon rise."

"That is odd," said the first owl, "I had assumed Snowy or Grey would come to tell us."

"Yes, I know it is. I just happened to be on a nearby tree and thought to anticipate their message." Under the penetrating gaze of three very fierce and large eyes, he began losing balance in the air.

"It is odd indeed," came a soft, threatening voice behind him. "And to think I was only just coming to inform my kin. You really are using this time to your advantage, meal."

The bird squawked, doing a complete circle in midair. When he saw it was Snowy (he had been eavesdropping on her and the other one), he was not so afraid. Just a little terrified.

"Snowy!" said the owls. "Is his report accurate?"

"Too accurate," she said. Her huge yellow eyes looked at the bird. "Did you honestly think we did not hear you?"

The bird floated down to a branch.

"I hoped," he mumbled.

"Since you are so bold—I saw you with that crow, impressive, by the way—can you please send the message to the surrounding horses and tell them to be on call for an advance?" Snowy said.

The bird shot up from the branch, excitement making his wings flap rapidly.

"Of course!" he said.

The owls watched the enthusiastic bird fly away.

"Interestingly, every creature is so easily situated to the new circumstances," said the first owl. He contemplated that puzzling thought for a second.

"Somethings readjust themselves accordingly. As the bird said, we are not programmed to do things out of the goodness of our hearts. We just do the right thing at the right time. This is that right time," said the second owl.

"Moon rise! We are very close. Do not lose track of the sun!" Snowy called out, flying away back to her post.

Chapter 43: Posts

The little blue grosbeak zipped across the sky to the horse pasture by the bubbling creek. "Excuse me," he said. He settled unobtrusively on the fence. The horses raised their heads from grazing.

"Yes?" the alpha mare asked.

"Well, I was instructed to pass on a message (at this point, he ruffled his feathers because he was feeling extra important) that you should be ready to move forward to Clement Valley after moonrise when called."

The troop of horses seemed singularly unmoved.

"Yes, yes," said one of the grazing horses, "we heard."

Now the little bird felt deflated.

"Do you think the owl knew that you already knew?" he was trying very hard to believe the best of his informant. The horses began to knicker.

"Of course, they knew," said another horse.

"Everyone for miles knows about this long-awaited battle," another horse added.

"Oh, don't feel so bad," said a feisty filly, "I am sure your help is invaluable."

"Yeah," said a cranky foal, pawing the ground, "if I were you, I would fly back to them and tell them you alerted us, and act like everything is cool, and not let them know you know you've been played. Dude, they've got nothing on you. You snapped at a crow!"

The bird thought about that and decided he agreed. It was true; he was bold. He was brave. Even confident enough to bicker with a crow.

"Well," he stated, feeling very important indeed, "I believe you are correct in your estimation of the caliber of creature I am. So, I will heed your advice and go forth to them casually proud."

The colt snorted. Whether from amusement or his generally crabby demeanor, no one could tell.

"That was entertaining," said the filly as the newly fluffed-up bird flew away.

"Come now," the alpha mare said, "that is enough fooling around with tiny creatures. Feed yourselves so you are prepared for the coming hours."

The horses silently grazed while hearing every word of their unflappable leader. Almost silent, that is.

"Why can't a guy eat in peace?" Grumbled the foal.

"What's wrong with being given guidance?" the unabashed filly challenged.

The alpha mare calmly walked up to them.

"You are young, I understand, but because you are young, you of all the horses need to listen. This is no easy thing we are going to do."

The colt began pawing the ground.

"I know," he said. "But I know we can do it."

"That's the spirit, my boy," the mare said.

The filly tossed her head.

"What about me?" she asked.

"And, of course, you," the mare said gently. "You are all a great troop. Why do you think they asked?"

"Because of you," said the filly, her eyes all but glowing.

The mare knickered.

The colt snorted.

"No, my dear, it is because we are a team," she said. Her solid, gentle demeanor made her a beloved leader.

"Okay, so now what?" asked the impatient (crabby) colt.

"We wait until we are called, dummy," said the filly. The mare nipped her gently.

"No need for name calling, especially at this time when we need to be together more than ever," the mare gently reprimanded her.

The colt looked at the alpha.

"That was literally the dorkiest thing I ever heard. We are always together because we are a troop of horses who will take a short walk to the other side of the road when we are called," he burst out.

The troop of at least twenty horses grazed calmly, but they did lift their heads at the outburst.

"Troublemaker," one of them said.

"Just wait until he comes to his whole stallion potential," said another.

"Maybe we'll get lucky, and they'll geld him."

"No way they'll do that," said a horse.

 "Do you see that guy's physique? And he's barely two!" concurred one of the mares.

The horses went back to grazing after pondering that reality.

"Listen here, young stallion," the alpha mare told the colt, "for so long as you are a colt, and I am the alpha, you will not disrupt the troops and the peace of the team like this. And do not mock the seriousness of the situation."

The colt was respectfully chastised. He lowered his head in acknowledgment.

"Much better," the mare said. "Horses do not fare well with cacophony noises, which is what we should expect.

That means we have to have an overwhelmingly clear and directed vision."

"I understand," said the colt.

"See that you do," she told him.

The mare looked at the colt, standing perfectly still, his head held high. She saw the muscularity of his chest and legs, anticipating his further growth.

The mare glimpsed, for a second, the promise of a strong and fair leader.

Chapter 44: The Other, Very, Very, Unexpected Visitor

He kept his breathing to a minimum. Which was very hard, considering his size. Creatures misunderstood him. They thought he was mean. Just because he was a bear. But in fact, he was very nice and felt very left out. He wanted to be a part of all the other animals in Clement Valley. Because when any of the animals saw him, they lowered their voices and ran and hid.

But he knows what happened to the baby deer and what the crows were planning. And he wanted desperately to be a part of the adventure. He lumbered as quietly as possible, which we already knew was probably not that quiet.

As the bear understood, whenever any of the forest creatures heard the bear, it made them afraid. The Clement Valley animals included. They were thrown into a quiet horror. GG simply passed out lying down in his cozy nook. JJ's heart was thumping so hard he was certain the bear could hear him through the walls. Moby was utterly paralyzed with an unknown fear. Knightley flew quietly from his perch, not knowing what their plans were supposed to be now. Maggie and Dune simply didn't move, waiting for him to pass.

What they did not expect was for their worst nightmare to simply plop down on the ground. Burying his face in his hands, he started wracking in sobs. Naturally, when he sobbed, it couldn't help but come out as a roar. A soft roar, but a roar nonetheless.

"I am not mean. I am nice!" he sobbed, well, roared. "Please give me a chance! The man shot me, and it did not hurt me, but it really hurt my feelings. I was just having breakfast. I couldn't resist the berries! But I didn't do anything to him!"

By now, he was nearly beside himself. His body was shaking so much from his sobs/roars he was making the ground tremble.

"What on earth?" muttered Grey from his perch.

"Yes," murmured Snowy, "how on earth do we deal with this extremely unnatural circumstance?"

"We have to convince him to move on so that the crows think he is just a bear passing through," Tolkien said, sighing.

They all stared at the sobbing, massive, overly emotional bear, wondering who among them was going to approach the mess of this unintentionally dangerous creature to talk to him.

"It should be a flyer," whispered GG, causing everyone to jump.

"Where on earth did you come from?" Snapped Kitty.

"We all came out," responded JJ, indicating Jake, Knightley, and Daisy.

"I'll tell him!" Daisy said, jumping excitedly.

"No, you most certainly will not," said Sun Flower. Her shoulders slumped in disappointment.

"I will," said Knightley.

"I am the most logical bearer of advice," he continued, "and can fly over to him silently. More importantly, I can stay above the reach of this emotional, unnatural mess."

By the end of his statement, he was looking at the weeping bear in disgust.

"What a disgrace," he muttered. Nearly as soon as he finished his statement, there was a low rumbling sound above the tree line.

"I hate those things!" shouted Sunny.

"Don't hate them," Knightley said, his tone satisfied, "because their timing is to our advantage."

"How?" asked GG.

"Because they will fly over the crows' nesting place and disrupt their sleeping preparation."

"That, combined with the threat of the bear," said Sun Flower, looking with disdain at the hiccupping bear, "will make them less prepared for our invasion."

The animals, as one, turned their gaze on the bear, who was wiping his face with his paws.

"So," said Kitty, "whose going to tell him? And what are they going to tell him?"

"How about me?" piped up Jake.

"Why you?" asked Sunny, staring at her previous victim through thin eyelids.

"You know how I used to live outside?" Jake did manage to keep his voice even despite Sunny's antics, "Well, I used to be by the Kramer's where Water Works here used to eat berries. And then defecate."

"I'm a dog," Tolkien said, turning his face away, "and they say canines are smelly, but they do not know that mice have no problem feasting on berries even in the middle of poop."

"Ew," said Sunny, licking her fur clean like she wanted to rid herself of the unsanitary image.

"Now I am grateful I did not eat you."

"Anyway," Jake continued, "I have that connection with him. That's why I should tell him."

"Thanks for taking the fall for the rest of us mus musculus, whatever, just mice, no reason to get all scientifically accurate now, is there?" said JJ in a low voice.

"Anytime," said Jake, grinning.

GG thought that if he was just quiet for once, no one would remember that he was a mouse. He was private about his mouse-dietary habits, which he knew most animals would find appalling.

"Since we are done with this ridiculous conversation—mice are called Mus musculus, by the way—," said Snowy, "which we none of us animals should be having, considering the understanding among our different families that we all eat to live following our honed instincts. What, pray tell, are you going to say to him?"

JJ rolled his eyes. "Show-off," he muttered and quickly looked away from Snowy.

"Something along the lines of Mr. Bear, we go way back to the days when you used to literally let loose your insides to fee-" Jake began before being interrupted by a chorus of objections.

"Don't finish, you disgusting animal!"

'What is wrong with your sense of privacy!?"

"Have you no dignity?!"

"These things are hidden for a reason!"

"Do not deface the sanctity of animal life!"

Jake was mildly taken aback.

"Sheesh, no need to get so prissy! We all understand ho…" Jake started to say.

"Just stop!" they shouted as one.

"Alright, alright," Jake said, "I will just tell him that we need him to-hey, what do we need him to do?"

Knightley glided down and perched on a weed.

"We need to tell him to walk across Archer's Field and take a left into the woods."

"That's it?"

"That beast is more than enough if he just pulls himself together," Kitty grumbled.

Jake straightened his shoulders bravely.

"Okay, I am going in." he tromped off toward the seated, tear-dripping, hiccupping menace of the forest.

Chapter 45: Into the Woods

The bear wiped his eyes (one last time. Then again, he always thought it was one last time.) When his vision cleared, he saw something moving in the grass. A mouse. His eyes brightened. His mouse!

"I can't believe you actually came to meet me!" His voice rang with enthusiasm. Usually, bears are never really happy, so when a bear voices anything, it usually leads to immediate evacuation.

The bear noticed that the mouse froze, and the furry little creature looked like it wanted to bolt. He stood and put his hands out in an attempt to be comforting.

"Oh, please do not do that, I am sure you are trying to be nice, but it is still terrifying," Jake pleaded with the bear.

The bear's eyes began to well. Jake ran up to the bear.

"No, really, please don't start the waterworks again," he told the bear.

"Really," he continued, "you see the rest of the animals? They don't understand you like I do, and I don't want them to misjudge you."

Jake's attempt at comfort had the entirely opposite effect.

"I can't believe how understanding you are!" he wailed. Jake buried his face in his hands.

What do I do now? he thought.

"Alright, my old comrade," Jake said as he inched closer to the distraught bear, "we need you now."

The bear wiped his eyes.

"You do? What do you need me to do?" he asked, still sniffling.

"You are our first distraction of The Battle. You have to walk through Archer's Field and into the forest, where the Crows are beginning to nest for the night. It should discombobulate them."

If it was at all possible, the bear stood taller.

If only he could see how utterly terrifying he is. Then again, it is very good that he can't! he thought emphatically.

"I will play my part!" he said, jumping up with enthusiasm (It was also a good thing everyone sat down as soon as he stood up). "Thank you so much for including me!"

He began to walk towards Archer's Field, almost as though he were rambling. Well, no matter how apparently undirected or meandering a bear looks when it moves, the reality is a bear's movement is always terrifying. Bears can't try to move slowly to be less intimidating. They are terrifying just because of what they could do if they so chose.

When he entered the woods, everything was still quiet. The sun was slowly sinking, and the woods were getting darker by the second. The diurnal animals were just returning home for sleep, and the nocturnal animals rested before their nightly rounds.

He looked up into the trees where the crows had their nests.

I wonder if they are scared, he thought.

If only he knew.

Chapter 46: Battle Plan Thwarted

The crows stared down at the bear. They were not frightened so much as they were unnerved. They kept waiting for him to pass through. Bears did not usually linger. But this one did.

"We can't move yet," said one crow. Like all animals in the vicinity of a bear respond, he spoke in a muted voice.

"Technically, we can," said another.

"He's not moving now," said a third, "but if we start to move, we could startle him, and who knows what he would do?"

"And we have babies!" scolded a protective mother.

"The helicopter flying over this afternoon certainly unsettled them enough as it is," another mother cackled.

"Well, that's all fine and dandy," said a male crow, "but now we cannot sound a general quarters alarm without letting the Clement Valley animals know that we are coming."

"What if this is a ruse and a part of their plot?" a young male crow asked.

There was a momentary silence from the murder before an indistinct dismissal of the youngster's null hypothesis.

"Ahh, my young ward," an older, decorated soldier sneered, "you are far too big for your unruffled feathers."

The young crow's eyes flashed in indignation, but he was cowed by the powerful crow.

"We will see," he said with a bent head.

None of them noticed the silent blue grosbeak seated on the ground beneath the brush.

Chapter 47: First Stage Executed

The night sky, aglow with the moon's first rays, made the setting deceptively peaceful. The Clement Valley animals were stationed. The ground was nearly entirely covered with mice in preparation for the second stage of the battle plan. Though they were eager to play their roles and emboldened by the understood truce, they could not help but feel extra cautious with the overwhelming presence of silent owls in the trees.

On the other hand, the unexpected presence of cats hiding in the underbrush loosened their tongues.

"I didn't know there would be cats!" whispered one mouse.

"We did know about the owls, but we were not informed about the cats!" responded another.

"Why should we feel more comfortable with the idea of owls, dimwit!"

"They are all equally horrifying, but we are still fighting on the same side," JJ interjected, trying to offer comfort in a daunting situation.

"That's easy for you to say, House Mouse. Most of us don't have the luxury of being house crumb fed," remarked a particularly rough-looking field mouse.

GG moved closer to JJ. The field mouse laughed.

"What? So now you are trying to be a force to be reckoned with?" the field mouse asked, his tone mocking.

"We are in a war!" Kitty said, standing and walking a few steps in front of the tense mouse-standoff.

"This means we have battle nerves. That's normal, but we can't fall apart now. Too much is at stake," she continued, wisely inserting her hard-earned words of wisdom.

"Mission accomplished. The crows are thrown off!" the tiny grosbeak stated as he flew into the scene of the altercation (Two mice standing face to face arguing is definitely a fight).

"And who put you in charge?" Kitty snapped. The bird flew in so low he startled the feisty goat.

Fluffing his feathers, the bird began boldly.

"Since I was sent to tell the team of horses and was informed that it was already a well-known fact across the entire valley," he paused to give the Clement animals a pointed look, "I decided to not give up despite what most creatures would consider low behavior... and flew into the

Murder, to see how things were developing."

The animals, in their shame, looked everywhere but at the bird.

Tolkien cleared his throat.

"We are so sorry that we did inadvertently, really, we did not know that we made you serve as a picket to check things out, but we knew no harm would come to you from that Alpha Mare's team," he said.

"It was a low action. You are very right," Knightley said, lowering his head apologetically. "We do most sincerely apologize."

"Yes, we all feel that way," Dune said, "but can you tell me about the young foal? Is he very grown?"

He was knocking the soil out of the way in agitation.

"Oh, stop being so insecure, Dune!" Maggie said, nipping him for good measure.

"Actually, the foal is a fine specimen," said the bird, "the mare told him he was turning into a formidable stallion."

Dune ran a ring around the paddock.

GG nudged JJ.

"I'm afraid he is going to accidentally call the other horses and agitate the owls," he said, casting his eyes towards the hidden, silent fleet of owls on the dark branches.

Sun Flower straightened.

"The horses will serve as our flanking maneuver, but will the mice be defiladed?" he asked. "You've been around a long time, right Knightley?" GG asked nervously.

"Yes, indeed, my little friend," the bat said.

"What is de-de-fellad and faking-an-muever?"

"Because of the context of the question, and the crow is asking about the mice, I can infer that de-fil-aded (he pronounced the word slowly) means protection. Flank (he split up the phrase this time) means the side of the horse, and maneuver means a planned move, so from that, I infer that they are speaking about the horses coming in literally from the left side of the property."

"Oh. What does infer mean?" GG asked.

"Infer means deduce."

"What does deduce mean?"

"Oh, for heaven's sake," JJ snapped at his cousin, "it means because you understand what is going on, you can guess what it means then."

Knightley felt his ability to understand more than almost everybody around him was being usurped.

"So, who will defend us?" asked Jake.

"Us."

The animals turned to look at the speaker. It was a sleek black cat. There was a colony of cats standing behind her. Sunny began to hiss.

She prowled over to the cats.

"I know some of you," she said, "and trust none of you!"

The cats began to creep closer to Sunny.

"She acts like a puppy," one murmured.

The other cats began to snicker. Tolkien bounded forward.

"And what's wrong with that," he growled. The sky was almost completely black, and the cats' eyes were glowing eerily.

"Nothing," one cat purred. "It is only amusing."

"We are not here to fight with anyone but the crows," said a tan cat. He seemed of wise temperament.

Suddenly, there was a ripple in the air coming from the Western Paddock.

"Mice," ordered the tan cat, "we will form a circle, so get in the middle!"

The mice, terrified and fighting their every instinct, began to run toward the cats.

Snowy and Grey took to the sky. The other owls followed suit. Like a silent wave, it seemed as though the tops of the trees were taking flight.

The scampering mice covered the ground. The cats prowled to encircle their charges. Dune was pacing restlessly, waiting to call out to the team.

And so began the long-awaited battle.

Chapter 48: Discord in the Enemy Ranks

"Coyotes," shouted one of the senior crows, "the Valley is awake and positioned, and we need enforcements!"

They watched the ground, filled with mice, easy for the taking. Except, were those cats providing a protective force around them? The crows were disoriented.

"Those are Owls flying up out of the trees!"

The crows stayed unmoving in the air. The sky blackened increasingly.

"What is this unholy sight?" Asked one crow.

"Owls and cats and mice are common predators and prey. I say we hunt."

"Don't be a fool. We have 12 generations of vengeance to exact!"

"How did we not anticipate this?" Asked a crow.

The young crow who had suggested this exact situation squawked triumphantly.

"Now will you hear me?" He asked. The gleam in his flashing black eyes left no room for objection.

"Rook. Do not think overstep your place," said the old veteran.

The young crow clucked softly.

"Young crows grow older. Like all things, every creature must fight to take its place," he said.

"Do not think to intimidate me!" The older bird said. He spread his wings to their greatest length, cawing.

"Stop this now!" A mother shouted. "We need to call the coyotes immediately!"

"I will call them," announced the belligerent crow. *Ahh, if only he knew the price he will pay for his arrogance.*

At the command of the senior crow, the crows left their roosts and flew up and into the sky of owls. The owls stayed their elevated places in the sky, unsheathing their claws. When the crows reached them, within seconds the owls began striking out, slashing with their razor sharp claws.

"Do not think we are alone!" Screamed a crow, as he scratched the owl's eye.

The owl within range lashed back, tearing the crow's wing.

"If you are this easy," the owl shouted, "I certainly hope not!"

Chapter 49: In the Heat of the Battle

The mice did a quick calculation of which situation was more dangerous.

On the one hand, they would be running in search of safety into a sanctuary of their universally acknowledged enemy.

On the other, equally terrifying hand, their runner-up enemies (basically every other known enemy to mice) were out to get them.

The Clement Valley cease-fire oath mitigated the danger of the cats. They quickly ran into the safe circle made of cats for their protection.

"This is insane!" GG shrieked, his heart racing as he pummeled through the grass.

Jake and JJ followed his frantic steps.

"I don't know who I am more afraid of," JJ said, "the cats or the outside mice who don't seem very nice."

"Don't be dumb," Jake said, "you should be way more afraid of the cats! And don't judge the outside mice just because they are different."

"Yeah, look at me!" piped up Daisy. "I am an outside mouse, and look how nice I turned out."

The three mice eyed her, disconcerted.

"If you are the example of outside mice," said JJ, "we should be terrified."

"Really," commiserated Jake, "you came in out of nowhere, have the protection of a crow, and are just way too happy!"

Daisy looked at them, her eyes filling with tears.

"You guys are mean!" she said, giving them her back.

"Oh, come on, Daisy," GG said gently, "we are all just scared."

JJ and Jake looked down, uncomfortable and ashamed.

"Listen," hissed the black cat, "can the three of you be quiet? Don't tempt me to break our covenant."

***

High above them, the mice watched the crows fly into the cloud of owls. The owls spread their wings protectively, letting loose hoots disconcerting the crows. They raised their curved claws, ready to attack.

Several of the crows were maimed, thick gashes hindering their flight. The crows retaliated, stabbing at the owls' eyes with their razor-sharp beaks.

The blackness of night was interrupted by the light of the rising moon. The cold glow of the moon's filtered sunlight cast a ghostly light on the battle below.

The hooting of the owls and the cawing of the crows filled the battle-strewn sky. The sights and sounds evoked terror in all present.

It seemed nothing could further incite horror until a cacophony of screams and shrieks was emitted from the black forest. The sourceless sound added to the general sense of dread.

***

"It's the coyotes!" shouted Snowy, neatly slicing through the wings of a crow.

"I would never have known," responded Grey sarcastically, plucking a torn wing off of himself as he spread his own wing to smack down another crow.

"Maybe," said another owl, "you should concentrate on fighting and not arguing over obvious facts!"

"Are we winning?" cried out another owl.

"We will only see in the end!" came a response. The owl then dove to attack a screaming coyote.

"There are so many!" a silver owl exclaimed as he whirled around to claw a crow. "Every time we defeat one, ten more arrive!"

***

On the ground, the sounds coming from the sky seemed to be getting closer. The howling of the coyotes convinced all of them—dogs, cats, and mice—that the coyotes were feasting.

Eyes wild with fear, Maggie and Dune began to buck and neigh.

"We are losing!" screamed GG. "They have already won, and the coyotes are coming!"

"Call the Team!" Kitty shouted at Dune.

Dune reared up, and let loose a shrill, loud, long neigh. Maggie's ears flattened to the back of her head as she paced nervously.

"I am scared," said Bambi, burrowing her head in her mother's side.

"I cannot argue that it is not a very alarming circumstance we find ourselves in," her mother told her, nuzzling Bambi, "but oddly enough, we are safe."

"Where is Tolkien?" asked Bambi.

Almost as if on cue, a rumbling noise crept up in the action zone. As the intensity increased, the trembling ground was mitigated only by the air clouded with dust from pounding hooves. The panting of the horses charging into the moonlit glow of the Western Pasture filled the mice and creatures on the ground with debilitating terror.

"Mama," whimpered Bambi, burrowing into her mother.

"Shhhh," the trembling mother told her daughter, trying to offer her protection despite the cawing crows, the hooting owls, the screaming coyotes, and now the galloping horses. "It's okay, don't worry, it's okay."

***

Dune and Maggie, wild with fear and adrenalin, watched the incoming stampede of horses in anticipation.

Maggie stood, eagerly awaiting her kind. "They certainly did the name of horses proud."

Naturally, Dune had a point to prove.

"I cannot wait to meet the Stallion!" he said, lying through his teeth.

"Well, here's your chance," Maggie said wryly.

Out of the cloud of dust, a resplendent horse- with carriage-perfect sculpted muscles and fiery eyes- came closer. Not too far after, a splendid mare followed in close suit.

Maggie and Dune watched in awe.

"He is wonderful!" exclaimed Maggie, with the direct purpose of riling Dune.

But he was not looking at him.

"Magnificent!" Dune said, unable to take his gaze off the head mare.

Maggie snorted and promptly bit Dune.

Dune reared.

"What was that for!?" Dune exclaimed, snorting.

"You little ingrate!"

It was as if there was no war going on full throttle around them. The raging battle in the sky, complete with an almost deafening sound, made no impression on the furious Maggie.

She reared up and kicked Dune, who was at this point trying to get away from his longtime companion.

"Magnificent!" she shrieked. "Do you know my name!?"

"Maggie!" Dune shouted, trying to figure out why she had seemingly lost her mind. "Of course, I know your name!"

"I am The Magnificent Bunny, from a long line of award-winning Magnificents!" she punctuated her statement with another kick.

Dune was running circles around Maggie, trying to keep out of her range.

"Just stop, Maggie! I was just saying she looks impressive—"

"Hold it right there, googly eyes," Maggie yelled.

"Just listen, please!" Dune pleaded.

"To what? Further descriptions?"

"No, just appreciate the beauty of our species. She just seems like a good leader," he said, his breath slowing as he saw Maggie was calming down.

Maggie neighed.

"Alright, maybe I was overly sensitive." she consented.

"Maybe?" Dune, still a little breathless from running laps around the paddock, looked at Maggie incredulously.

He jumped back, whinnying when a dead crow fell at his hooves.

"What is wrong with the two of you?"

Maggie and Dune were startled by the crisp, disapproving question.

"The sky is exploding, the coyotes are a breath away, and we are in the middle of a raging battle!" said the head mare, shaking her head in agitation.

Dune was rendered speechless. Maggie bristled.

"Neighbor," Maggie said, "we are aware. We called you and your team."

The head mare looked at Maggie; patience and wisdom radiated from her penetrating gaze. Maggie squirmed.

"Yes," the head mare said, "you wisely did so. Now, we need to engage in this long-awaited battle."

Maggie squashed her defensive pride.

"In your estimation, how close do you think the coyotes are?"

"The crows sent a messenger to them from the Western Pasture, and the messenger flew North East, according to the Grosbeak."

"You know him?" asked Dune, and then became horrified at his boldness.

"Yes," the head mare said. "His size is quite useful."

"We know that means they are close enough to pounce when more birds start to fall," said the stallion, kicking the dead crow with his hoof.

Dune stiffened.

"Even though he is the enemy, we honor the rights of the dead and treat them respectfully," Dune said.

He closed the short distance between himself and the stallion. Head to head, the horses stood, unmoving. Finally, the stallion lowered his head in acceptance.

"I apologize. You are right." the stallion said.

"Though Dune is considerably younger than me, he is old enough for you to take as a mentor," noted the head mare. She looked at Dune, assessing him.

"I did not know there was another stallion so close by," she added.

"A cryptorchid stallion," said Maggie. She was worried. *Dune, a stallion? I raised him. He is not a stallion! He cannot handle that psychological confusion*, she thought.

"Formidable, nonetheless," said the head mare.

That is not the bearing of your average Crypto. Maggie cannot see how much of her stalwart and unchallenged confidence Dune has imbibed, the head mare thought.

Dune, on the other hand, was on cloud nine.

I knew I was more than just a crypto! This head mare, with a stallion in her team, thinks I am a stallion!

"I suggest we move towards the North East side of the pasture," continued the head mare.

"Should we charge?" asked the stallion, nearly prancing.

"No, we should definitely not!" Kitty screeched, coming from out of nowhere.

The horses were spooked – all twenty-seven of them.

The resulting hysteria added immeasurably to the terror the screaming night sky was evoking.

Bambi crouched by the fence.

"Mama, don't do it!" her mother was going to the herd of horses to calm them.

"If it gets too dangerous, I'll just come right back."

Gracefully and serenely, the doe glided to the pond, where the spooked horses were.

"What are you doing?" Kitty asked.

"It is known that most goats cause calmness amongst horses," the deer said.

Kitty was indignant.

"I will have you know—" she started to say.

The doe gently put her face next to Kitty's.

"But you have such a hefty load to carry on the farm at this time, especially." she nuzzled Kitty.

"That's true," said Kitty, "and nobody sees it!" she lifted her head, finally feeling vindicated.

The doe walked near the horses, zoned in on a young filly, and decided to start from there.

The filly was at the edge of the herd. The doe quietly stood next to her.

"Are you scared?" she asked the filly.

The filly, eyes wide with fear, turned her head towards the doe.

"Yes, I am! I cannot tell what is happening," the filly exclaimed.

"We do find ourselves in a very dangerous situation. It is a war, defending the Clement Valley way."

The filly looked at her, almost as if just noticing her. Her eyes locked at the doe.

"It would be funny if I wasn't so scared. We are in the middle of a war, but I feel much calmer just looking at you," said the filly.

"I am happy to hear that," said the doe. "Usually, the goats have that effect on horses, but right now, Kitty has too much to do."

The filly looked down, saying shyly, "I like you."

The sense of calm began to spread among the rest of the horses.

***

"The doe certainly did the trick," said Maggie.

"Yes, indeed," said the lead mare, "and quite on time, if I may add."

"Now, we should start talking about what we will do," said Dune.

"We know these coyotes," said the stallion, "and they are a particularly bad lot."

"Yes!" Dune agreed emphatically. "They cross boundaries of even common scavenger laws!"

"There is a reason," said the lead mare. "Do not forget that they were infected two decades ago."

"How?" asked Maggie.

"One of them was infected with the monstrous illness, and she delivered a litter of puppies who carried that infection," said the mare.

"Yes, of course," said Maggie nodding. "That would explain their brutal massacring of Rumor."

"He was a hero," said Dune.

"How?" asked the eager young stallion.

"He defended his family, even when he was mortally wounded," Dune said.

"He drew them away from the house and his boy." said Maggie.

"And he killed their leader," Dune added.

"So, they come with a vengeance of their own," the lead mare said.

"Their crow cohorts were part of his murder, and crows are known for their vengeful behavior that carries down through generations," explained Dune.

Now the young stallion was staring, starry-eyed, at Dune.

"So now, what do we do?" he asked, eagerly pawing the ground.

"No one can take on coyotes like head mares." the lead mare swished her tale sharply. With that, she plodded over to Maggie. "And there are two of us."

Maggie tossed her mane.

"Let us lead our teams and stampede their grounds!" Maggie exclaimed.

Chapter 50: The Coyotes

Watching their quarry through the tangle of branches, the coyotes howled.

How it went was like this. The first coyote howled, the second caught the signal and sounded the alarm, and then the third screamed. Within minutes, every coyote in the area took up the cry. The sinister wailing filled the dark, shadowy woods.

"Is it finally going to happen? Will we finally get our revenge?" the coyote asked, saliva dripping from his mouth as he licked his lips.

His mangy companion let out an ear-splitting scream, his snout pointing to the sky, letting his wail trail off.

"It has been too long, but yes, we will finally get our vengeance!" he said, prowling around the trees.

The coyote pack walked close to the ground. Not only were they hunting, but were also driven by animosity towards Clement Valley dogs. Rumor killed their alpha. Their alpha had to be avenged. And who better to take the fall than Tolkien!

The timing was perfect. In the midst of a battle, where many should die, the death of Tolkien would be a natural outsome of the war. One segment of the coyote pack did the unnerving howling, and the other silently skulked across the grounds in search of the ideal place and time to kill Tolkien.

Chapter 51: Beary in a Barrel

Beary trudged through the forest.

"All I did was stand under the crow's nests. I wonder if I really helped," he questioned.

He lifted his head, trying to hear.

"There is certainly a lot of cawing and hooting, and I think I heard horses also," he contemplated.

"But does that mean I helped? Maybe I should go and see for myself." with that, his steps became more purposeful.

He was at the top of the ridge now but could not see what was happening down below. Suddenly, he smelled something.

"Sap!" instantly, all thoughts of the battle below flew out of his mind.

"This tree!" he grabbed the tree as if to crack it in half until he noticed something else. A barrel filled with sap!

He lowered his head to the barrel.

"Oh, how perfect! All right here!"

He blissfully began to lap up the freshly tapped sap. He ate and ate and ate until he reached the bottom of the pail.

"Just this last droplet!" he hollered, raising his head up.

Now, remember, his head was still in the pail. He could not see, so he did not notice the log right in front of him. So, of course, he tripped.

"The droplet! Wait! Wait! Wait! Hold on! Slow down! Waaaaaaiiiiiit!"

And down he rolled, over logs, over bushes, and into trees.

The coyotes heard the tremendous crashes of the falling trees.

"That's a bear!"

Then they started to mock the sight of the rolling bear, his head in a sap barrel.

"Good! One less enemy for us!" The coyote said.

The coyote spoke too soon, though. The barrel-headed bear bumped into an oddly angled rock that sent him shooting off directly in the line of the coyotes. Beary accidentally grabbed the coyote's tail, twirling him through the air as he plummeted down the hill.

The coyotes' jeering laughter turned into shrieks of panic. They watched and began to run away as Beary hurtled towards them, whirling a coyote over his head.

Beary's rolling finally slowed.

"Phew," he said, as he managed to extricate his head from the pail, not noticing the legion of flat coyotes behind him, "It's a good thing I did not hurt anything!"

Chapter 52: Tolkien's 6th sense

The howling of the coyotes always unsettled Tolkien. Amid all the battle noises, his blood already running hot with fear and blood lust, it now filled him with anger.

"Sunny!" he hollered, "I am going into the coyotes!"

"You're crazy!" she shrieked, "we need you here!"

"No, you don't," he said, bounding off, "you have your cat family. And you're not even a Clement animal! They are your family, the Ken's Lane family, and they are doing great!"

"Wait! You are a real Clement animal, so you are more my Ken's Lane family's family, which makes you my family! I don't even like cats anymore!" her hysterical shouts faded into the general madness of war. Tolkien was long gone.

***

As he tore down the field, his blood rushing loudly in his ears, he had one clear thought: *I will find the coyotes who killed Rumor.* Coyotes and crows held onto their revenge, passing it down through generations. Certainly, the name Rumor was running on their tongues on this bloody field.

Suddenly, he stopped short. His nose smelled something different. *A coyote, yes. But why different? Was it old? A little, but not very. Sick? Yes, its blood was infected. This was the one.* Tolkien prowled closer to the ground.

"You have come to me to do what you did to Rumor," Tolkien said, "but you will not succeed."

The alpha coyote laughed.

"Do you think I am alone, Dog?" he said, stepping out from behind the bramble.

Tolkien paused an inch before the alpha.

"No," Tolkien said, "but I think every leader runs his time, and then a new leader takes his place."

"You are a fool! No one will take my place until I die, and no one will kill me!" the alpha shrieked.

Now Tolkien laughed softly.

"Arrogance always comes before the fall. And you made yourself an enemy amongst your ranks as the alpha crow did."

The coyote began to feel uncomfortable.

"Of course, I did not!" he said.

"And now the young crow and the young coyote are working in cohorts to finish off the old generation, but I will save them the trouble," said Tolkien.

"Never!"

"Yes, and they believe they will serve justice and prove themselves by killing me, but do they not know that the mutilating of the innocent will never go unrequited? And they do not know what I have waiting for them!"

He finished that last foreboding threat and lunged at the evil coyote, sinking his teeth into his jugular vein.

Chapter 53: Justice Served

What he came upon after the innocent life of Rumor was avenged was almost as terrifying as the coyote howls. A path of flattened coyotes made him slow his pace.

"What on earth?" he murmured. "How did this happen? I meant for justice to be sought, but I could never have imagined this!"

He put his nose down to the ground and began following the scent.

"Beary!" He said. "I didn't know he had it in him."

"Had what in me?" Beary asked. Tolkien jumped half a mile.

"Beary, you scared me! And I am a dog who hears 7 times better than most creatures!" Tolkien growled.

Beary thought about that.

"Well, I hear pretty good, too," he said, "'But I wonder how many times better. Maybe 7, too. Or 8. Maybe 4." he stared off into the distance as he wondered. Tolkien covered his eyes. He couldn't handle this odd mammal!

"Nice work with those coyotes, though," Tolkien told him, trying to feel more positively about Beary. He clapped

Beary on his...well, leg with his paw. Beary's shoulder was far too high.

"Yes, they did become quiet very quickly," he chuckled. "They must have heard me running. They did not know I would never hurt them even though they deserved it!"

My goodness, he doesn't know. I won't tell him. He would start roaring tears, Tolkien thought, but then paused. *Maybe I should. That might scare off the other creatures. Then again, it might hurt him too much. Maybe that's what he needs to make him normal. What am I thinking? He would squash me then!*

"Yes," Tolkien said, content to leave Beary to his strange ways, "I am sure that would have never occurred to their soundly sleeping corpses. I mean bodies." He amended when he saw Beary start.

"What is that?" Beary asked.

"What?" asked Tolkien, his ears pointing straight up.

"That!" The bear shouted, pointing upwards. Tolkien looked up and saw a gigantic, black cloud.

Tolkien sniffed.

"Too far up, and I can't single out the smell from the other flying creatures," Tolkien said.

"I can," Beary stated, scratching his head. "They are bats."

Tolkien whined.

"That is not part of the plan. Knightley said he would never call them!"

Chapter 54: The Silent Warriors

Knightley stared at the cloud of bats in the sky.

"I do not believe it," he said.

Knightley was torn between joy, confusion, and horror. *Should he fly up to them?* he snorted. *To what? Welcome them?* An image of a conversation with them in the war-torn sky flickered in his mind:

"I am so glad to see you finally! Please excuse the falling crow and duck your head! An owl is zooming by."

As he stared at the sky, one bat broke from the flock.

Knightley spread his wings and went to meet the bat midway.

"My dear bat! What are you doing here?" he asked, his eyes wide in surprise.

"My old friend!" the other bat chuckled.

"I am surprised you still remember me, now that you have a new-found companion," the old friend said.

"Come now," Knightley said, trying to lead the bat toward safety. "It is most certainly not the place and barely even the time for reminiscing."

His statement was punctuated by the deathly caw of a falling crow. While he was saying that, the bat cloud came lower. Suddenly, Knightley and his friend were shielded from the dangers of the sky.

Knightley could hardly believe it. Amidst the chaos of war, he saw his oldest friend. He could not process the clash of his two worlds. Before he became a house bat, he was a bat from a community that prided itself in never finding refuge in anything but a tree!

"How did you come by me?" Knightley asked.

His friend laughed softly, a sound that opposed the havoc surrounding them.

"We do not forget our own, even when they disappear," the bat said.

"We got word," Knightley's friend continued serenely, "or echo of the attack made on you by the squirrel and the subsequent rescue made by your friend. So, we felt secure that you would be taken care of. That was why we did not come for you."

"I assumed so," said Knightley, "and was glad not to break our family's outside ways. But tell me, what brought everyone here? That is not our way."

"That is true," said his friend, "but nor is it our way to not offer protection to one of our own, especially in a time of battle for a noble cause."

Knightley nodded. *Bats, being as they are dignified, would never sit by and not engage in something they considered noble.*

"When did you decide to come?" He asked.

"During our nightly gathering, we shared news of the coming battle and your role in it. We decided it was time to break our pattern this once."

"Let me introduce you to my house family," Knightley told him.

***

The mice—JJ, GG, and Jake—were looking at Knightley and another bat coming down towards them. Their guardians were prowling restlessly.

"Who is that? What is Knightley doing?" GG asked.

"It is really strange, but I think it must be help!" JJ exclaimed.

"Knightley said his family would never come," Jake said. He busied himself by concentrating on the cats, so no one would be able to tell how insecure he was feeling.

"You look like I just swallowed you," said a cat, inching closer to him.

"What? Cat got your tongue?" the prowling cats started snickering.

"Oh, no," one slinking cat declared. "That's not it! You are jealous. You are scared he will replace you. Cats understand these things," she said, licking her paw.

Jake moved away. *No wonder why mice are afraid of cats,* he thought morosely. *How did she know? Wait, am I?*

"Jake!" said Knightley. His friend settled next to him on a weed.

"This is my very old friend. Though he is considerably younger than me, we used to converse during communion when our echolocators were off," he explained.

The other bat settled lightly between Jake and Knightley.

"Please, just let me say sorry on behalf of all bats, Jake," he said, "that you have to deal with his...well...his ridiculous vocabulary and his overwhelming sense of self."

Jake opened his eyes so wide they were about to pop out. Then he began to laugh loudly, nearly drowning out the sound of the battle.

"Really, friend," said Knightley, "was that necessary? And Jake, there is no need to laugh. We are at war, for heaven's sake!"

JJ and GG watched curiously.

"Why don't you introduce us, Knightley?" GG asked. He crossed his arms over his chest and winced. "I don't know why I keep doing that. It hurts!"

"Now is neither the time nor place. I promise when this is over," he said, casting his glance to the raging sky, "we will do the honors."

"Yes," said the friend, "now, let us talk about what we bats intend to do."

"What?" asked Jake.

"Just be bats," said Sunny. "That usually takes care of it."

Just one bat and she could not stop her fur from standing on end. A whole flock of them was about to make her fur fall off.

Knightley's old friend looked warily at her.

"I should not be surprised with this very oxymoronic companionship," he said. "Strange things do seem to happen here in Clement Valley."

"Yes, yes," said Kitty, who stomped over to take her place, once again, understood, "they do. But what are you going to do?"

Bambi and her mother bounded over.

"Will you help it end soon?" Bambi asked.

"We will bite them," the bat said matter-of-factly.

The animals stood silently, waiting for details.

"And then what?" said Daisy.

"Yes, indeed, considering how rare it is for a bat bite to get an animal sick," said Sunflower.

"Yes, one bite will not do it. But a flock of bites will do the trick," said Knightley's old friend.

"You will swarm them!" Knightley exclaimed. "Very good planning."

"That would work," Sun Flower said, nodding in agreement.

"When?" JJ asked.

The bat turned to Knightley.

"Whenever our fierce leader commands."

The night sky was like a snuffed candle. It was the blackest part of the night, heralding the Sun's gentle entrance. Daylight was coming.

"Now," said Knightley.

"Now what?" GG piped up.

Knightley's friend lifted his wings in a salute. Before he returned to tell the other bats to attack, he stopped.

"Jake," he called out. Jake lifted his head.

"Yes?" Jake said.

"Do not worry. And thank you. Knightley could not have asked for a better friend. I do not think he will leave his home ever."

"Oh, would you look at that," the intrusive cat purred, "now you can relax. You won."

Jake did not want to show his happiness to the cat, but he was elated. As soon as he saw the bats, he was scared that Knightley would return to his family. He did not like seeing himself jealous or overly attached to any creature.

Oh my God. She was so right! Wait. What am I doing? She is the enemy!

As Jake battled his conflicting emotions, the owls felt an imperceptible flutter in the air.

"What is that?" asked Grey.

Snow swiveled her head, looking through the flying and falling bodies around her. She inhaled sharply.

"Bats!" she said.

"Bats? What brought them out of their enclave?"

Snowy started laughing.

"Do not forget their lasting memories, or they have one of their own here!"

The crows heard the owl chatter in the midst of the noise.

"Bats!" said one crow snidely. "What are they going to do? Give us rabies?"

"No," came a soft voice behind him, "we have a mission. All two thousand of us will only fly in and bite the crows. Whether or not they will get rabies depends on how precise our bites are." "It can be difficult to reach the eyes. The material point, though, is to disrupt your flow."

At Knightley's command, the bats swarmed in. They began biting at large. The crows looked like a body of water during a wind storm. Jumping with every bite, they began spreading through the lightning sky in every direction.

"Look!" said Jake excitedly. "The crows are leaving! Knightley is brilliant!"

"Yes," said Sun Flower, "he is indeed."

"I like him, too," said Daisy, scampering over to Sun Flower.

"Well," said Sun Flower, clearing his throat, "I am glad you are safe now, Daisy."

"Is it over?" GG asked.

"I think it is," said Tolkien, who came bounding over.

"Tolkien!" Bambi exclaimed. She ran and burrowed her head in Tolkien's fur. Tolkien always loved the attention and stood stock still to enjoy the moment.

"Oh," said Tolkien, abruptly, remembering. "Beary wants to know if he can come out now."

The Clement Valley animals froze. All the horses' ears stood straight up.

The stallion began pawing the ground. He turned his head toward Dune.

"What do we do now?" The white of the stallion's eyes were like beacons.

Well, wouldn't you know? He is terrified, even though he is a stallion!

"I would not object, as he has shown himself to be a very sensitive bear who does not act as bears normally do."

Maggie, as usual, bit Dune. He jumped.

"Why do you keep doing that!?" he said, bucking.

"You know, in the Equine world, the mares dictate how the team responds," Maggie said.

"And we think he is a manageable bear," said the head mare, laughing.

"Well, he makes me nervous," GG said.

"Understandable," JJ said. "He could accidentally squash us just by walking."

Or rolling, thought Tolkien, remembering the smashed coyotes.

"That's true, but he seems very caring," chirped Daisy cheerfully.

"No one is that caring," murmured Sunny. Her head shot up suddenly.

"Where are they?" she asked sharply.

"Who?" said Tolkien. "Do you mean the cats? They just slinked off when the bats came along."

"Good riddance," said Sunny.

"No need to be so traitorous," said Tolkien.

"I, for one, am very relieved," said JJ.

"You are relieved?" said Jake laughing. "At least Sunny and I have an understanding now. Even though my time with Sunny only showed me how terrible cats can be."

"Why so certain that we have an understanding?" Sunny asked, prowling towards Jake.

Jake looked Sunny straight in the eyes.

"Because of Tolkien."

Sunny sniffed and walked away. JJ, GG, Moby, and Jake walked across the field and slipped under the door. In their cozy little crevice in the rocks, they sat down.

"Well, that happened," said JJ.

"And I didn't even see a hawk," Moby said. His shoulders slumped forlornly.

"If you miss him that dearly my boy," Knightley said, "feel free to speak with me. I do not need human words to express myself."

Jake rolled his eyes and clapped Moby on the back. Moby, naturally, propelled forward.

"Sorry, little guy," Jake said, apologizing on behalf of his mentor.

GG crossed his hands behind his head and leaned back.

"That really hurts!" GG shouted. "It looks so relaxing when Tolkien's boy does it!"

JJ laughed.

"When are you going to stop doing what his boy does?" Jake asked, scampering up the rocks, seeking the comfort of his closet.

"Most probably when you begin to change your vocabulary to speech showing the effects of my stellar example!" Knightley said, flying cautiously up the narrow space.

Epilogue

Clement Valley Proper

The Clement Valley family drove up the driveway.

"Something seems different," said Tolkien's boy.

"Yeah, doesn't it?" his sister said.

"I don't see anything different," said their mother.

Tolkien came bounding up to his boy.

"How are you, boy?" his boy said to his dog before he walked to the house. All of a sudden, he stopped short.

"Baba!" he shouted.

"There is a huge paw print here!"

Out On Ken Lane

"Do you notice anything different?" The oldest brother asked the twins.

"No," they stated.

The 10 siblings sat in front of the huge living room window on the top floor.

"We do," said the five other siblings.

It looks like there are places where lots of things were happening," said the third youngest sister.

"That's silly. What do you mean, 'lots of things?" said her youngest brother.

"Look!" Shouted her older brother (not the oldest). They all looked out of the window.

"It's a flying pink elephant!"